Reading Comprehension

Resource Material for Teachers and Parents

Reading Comprehension

The Components of Reading
Resource Material for Teachers and Parents

Yvonne Luteania Simon, Ed.D.

ISBN: 978-1-62550-568-2 (PB)

Printed in the United States of America by Llumina Press

978-160594-897-3 (PB) 2012
Library of Congress Control Number: 2012906699

TABLE OF CONTENTS

Overview

The purpose of this article is to discuss the foundation and concepts that are very important and necessary to achieve the level of reading comprehension. They are print concepts, oral language development, phonemic awareness, phonics, fluency, vocabulary, and text comprehension. These are the necessary components for students to master so that they will be able to become fluent readers. Besides the above-mentioned components for improving reading comprehension, technology and computer reading programs are also equally important. (National Reading Panel 2000). Teaching practice that succeeds in developing deep understanding of challenging contents such as teaching young children to read is highly complex. This process maintains a Socratic dialogue between students and subjects, allowing neither to overwhelm the other. Such teaching paradigms press for mastery of content in ways that enable students to apply their learning and connect it to other knowledge as they develop proficient performances in the field of study. Words are our tools to communicate with others, as well as explore and analyze the world around us. Therefore, it stands to reason that children with a limited vocabulary will be handicapped in their educational progress. The most obvious effect of an underdeveloped vocabulary will be seen in poor reading comprehension, as children struggle to extract meaning from reading passages. Well-developed vocabulary and reading comprehension skills are central to success on the standardized **tests** used in most states. In many cases, students' promotion to higher grades is directly at stake. Vocabulary appears in two main ways:1) Reading questions that directly test vocabulary 2) Comprehension questions that require strong vocabulary knowledge is not automatic and, regardless of family background, children require support in learning to read and developing strong reading skills. As adults, most of us have forgotten how much work and skill goes in to learning to read. (Calkins, 2001). Learning to read starts with building a language-rich environment for your child. This forms a solid foundation on which reading skills including decoding, fluency, vocabulary, and comprehension are based Things such as practicing nursery rhymes, and playing letter and word games and later letting your child read aloud help develop phonemic awareness and letter-sound knowledge early on. Tutoring or structured computer programs can also effectively reinforce these skills. Based on an understanding of phonemic (or phonological) awareness and basic print concepts, children are ready to learn phonics and to start decoding words. Learning to read is like climbing up a ladder. Each step forward is based on the previous step. The Reading Comprehension pyramid shows the steps in this progress. Furthermore, students will necessarily come to any learning experience with different learning strategies and prior experiences. How do we help students struggle with all these various strategies? Support and encourage them. Effortful decoding is a necessary step to sight recognition. You can say, "I know reading is tough right now, but this is how you learn new words." Ask students to reread each sentence that requires unusual decoding effort. Successful teachers must know how to create experiences that allow students access ideas in a variety of ways, nevertheless, always press for deeper and more disciplined understanding. Additionally, this kind of teaching children how to read and comprehend is purposeful and may be highly structured, but it is also inevitably improvisational. Since real understanding is always hard won, and human beings bring different mixes of abilities and insights to the task, there is no prepackaged set of steps or lessons that will secure understanding for every learner in the same manner. Teachers have to bring a great deal of knowledge and analytic ability to the task of developing understanding with their students in this specific endeavors; teach students how to read. Therefore, based on the teacher's knowledge and analytical ability, all students will understand and apply the knowledge of sounds, letters, and words in written English to become independent and fluent readers, and will read a variety of materials and texts with fluency and comprehension. A primary reading goal is for students of all grades to read independently with fluency and comprehension so that they become lifelong readers and learners. In order to achieve this goal, students benefit from "daily opportunities to read books they choose for themselves, for their own purposes, and their own pleasures" (Calkins, 2001). Students should read grade-level appropriate or more challenging classic and contemporary literature and informational readings, both self-selected and assigned. In order to grow as readers and deepen their understanding of texts, students need many opportunities to think about, talk about, and write about the texts they are reading. A diversity of reading material (including fiction and nonfiction) provides students with opportunities to grow intellectually, emotionally, and socially as they consider universal themes, diverse cultures and perspectives, and the common aspects of human existence.

In early reading instruction (preK-2), children need rich experiences with oral language and learning about sounds, letters and words, and their relationships. Phonemic awareness, knowledge of the relationships between sounds and letters, and an understanding of the features of written English texts are essential to beginning reading. Direct systematic phonics instruction enables many students to develop their knowledge of phonics, and provides a bridge to apply this knowledge in becoming independent and fluent readers. Systematic phonics instruction typically involves explicitly teaching students a pre-specified set of letter-sound relations and having students read text that provides practice using these relations to decode words (National Reading Panel, 2000). Additionally, direct instruction and time to practice these skills should be provided in comprehension, strategy, reading fluency, and vocabulary development at all grade levels. It is important to help students become fluent readers in the early years, and then help them expand their literacy abilities as they progress through the middle and high school grades. The reading process requires readers to respond to texts, both personally and critically, and relate prior knowledge and personal experiences to written texts. Students apply literal, inferential, and critical comprehension strategies before, during, and after reading to examine, construct, and extend meaning. In becoming fluent readers, students must draw on the word meaning and sentence structure of text and sound/symbol relationships, and use these cueing systems interchangeably in order to comprehend and gain meaning. Students need to recognize that what they hear, speak, write, and view contributes to the content and quality of their reading experiences.

The National Reading Panel (NICHD 2000) published its research results and recommendations in a report entitled Teaching Children to Read: An evidenced-Based Assessment of the Scientific Research Literature on Reading and its implications for Reading Instruction. This national report presented five key literacy topics: phonemic awareness, phonics, fluency, vocabulary and text comprehension that should be included in daily literacy instruction. Although the National Reading Panel and its published report have enthused much controversy (Allington 2002; Ehri and Stahl 2001; Garan 2001; Smith 2003; Yatvin 2002), state departments of education have based their state frameworks and tests on the tenets of this panel's research. Additionally, the federal government has sponsored the No Child Left Behind (NCLB) legislation, which focuses on state test scores and the annual progress all students make on each state assessment (Ryan and Cooper 2004; Sturrock 2003). To provide effective and relevant literacy instruction, a teacher should be aware of the National Reading Panel's report, the controversy surrounding it, state standards, high-stakes testing, and the influence that state standards and national directives have on a school district's literacy curriculum.

The written English language is based on the alphabetic principle that means letters are used to represent sounds. In a perfect alphabet, only one letter represents only one sound, and so readers can pronounce any written word by simply associating sounds with letters (Fox 2004). However, the English alphabet is not perfect. Consequently, one letter can represent one sound; two or more letters can represent one sound; a silent final vowel can affect the sound of the medial vowel; and many words have letters that are not sounded.

ACKNOWLEDGEMENTS

If I were to acknowledge all the educators throughout the world, the ones who inspired students to read and write, and the ones who challenged students to be the best that they can be, there would be a list of names that would be too enormous to include in this book. I could fill another volume with the many students and colleagues from whom I have gathered ideas and with whom I have shared reading comprehension activities with. However, some of the noted authors are named in the text. They are quoted and cited for the unfolding learning experiences presented here. I hope they will accept my thanks for their inspiration and teachings

ON TRACK

READER PREPARED

FOR SUCCESS

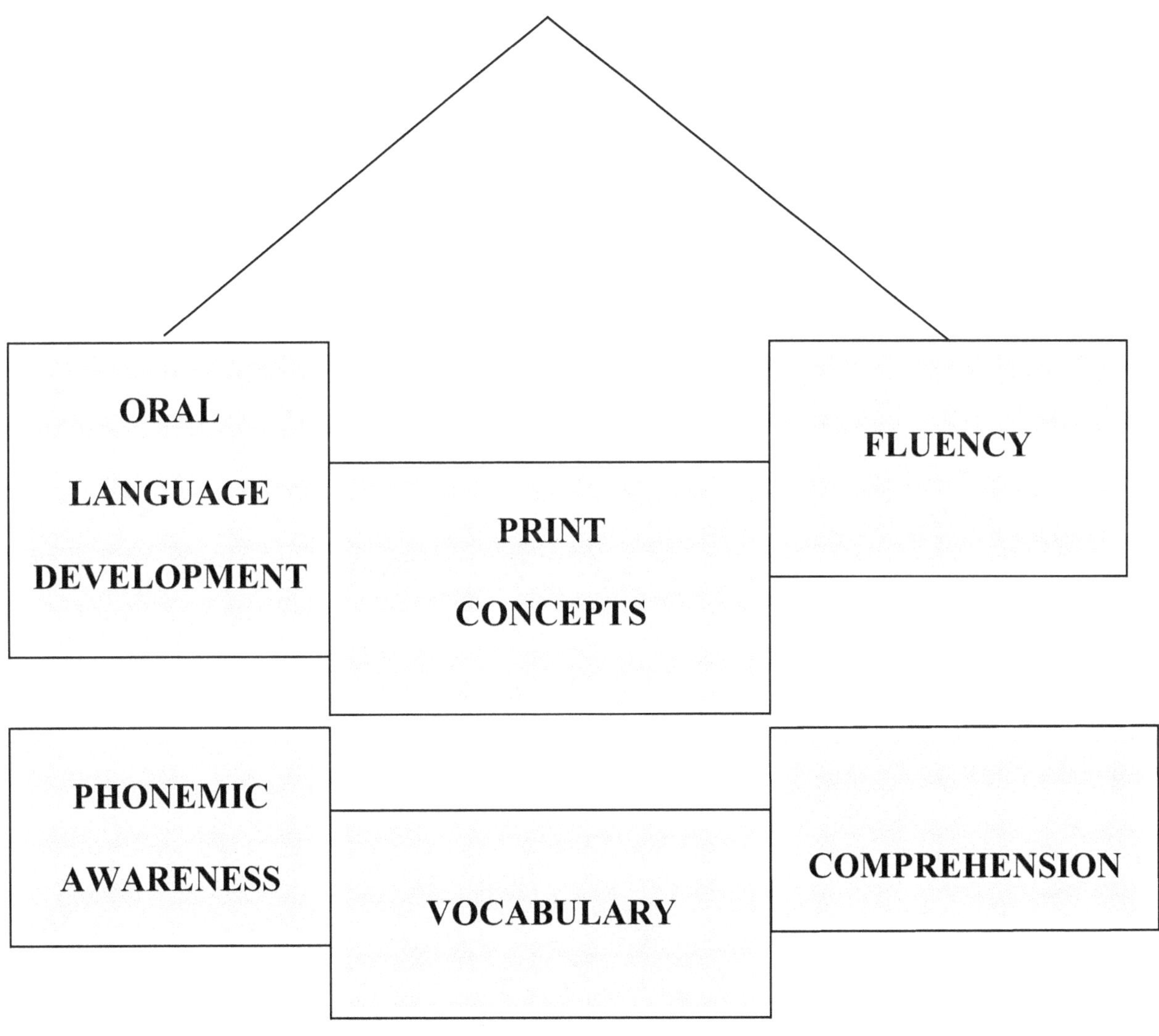

CHAPTER I

ORAL LANGUAGE DEVELOPMENT

Reading readiness has been defined as the point at which a person is ready to learn to read and the time during which a person transitions from being a non-reader into a reader. Other terms for reading readiness include early literacy and emergent reading.

Children begin to learn pre-reading skills at birth while they listen to the speech around them. In order to learn to read, a child must first have knowledge of the oral language. According to the Ontario Government (2003), the acquisition of language is natural, but the process of learning to read is not - reading must be taught. This belief contradicts basic language philosophy, which states that children learn to read while they learn to speak. The Ontario Government (2003) also believes that reading is the foundation for success, and that those children who struggle with reading in grades 1-3 are at a disadvantage in terms of academic success, compared to those children who are not struggling.

The development of oral language is one of the child's most natural, and impressive, accomplishments. This discussion presents processes and mechanics of language development along with implications for practices (Gambrell, 2004). Oral language is a fundamental element of literacy in the development of oral language. Extensions related to the manipulatives were integrated throughout the curriculum The reading standard incorporates the following literacy components throughout the grades and takes into consideration individual learning differences and student motivation. Specific to reading, speaking, and listening standards are oral language print concept, phonemic awareness, phonics, fluency, vocabulary and comprehension Teachers encourage students' language development through informal and guided conversations by asking questions, and by providing opportunities for students to explain their learning or thinking. Teachers model and discuss vocabulary and formal English grammar while reading, writing, or sharing experiences, without correcting or evaluating student's speech patterns.

Oral language is crucial to a child's literacy development, including listening, speaking, reading, and writing skills. While the culture of the child influences the patterns of language, the school environment can enable children to refine its use. As children enter school, they bring diverse levels of language acquisition to the learning process. Therefore, teachers face the challenge of meeting the individual needs of each language learner, as well as discerning which methods work most effectively in enhancing language development. Conflicting messages regarding methodology in oral language development have resulted in a heavy reliance on programs and "quick fixes," inhibiting the use of authentic, contextualized language experiences in classrooms

Most recently, the No Child Left Behind Act of 2001 (NCLB) has placed an overemphasis on using standardized means of testing children, while holding schools accountable for systematic progress during the year. Although NCLB emphasizes scientific research-based teaching methods, many of these methods primarily promote the teaching of discrete pieces of information and a fragmented curriculum (Aldridge, 2003). The development of oral language, which ultimately affects all aspects of curriculum, has been relegated to a mere incidental byproduct of many classrooms, in order to allow time to drill children on test items. Additionally, as curriculum is pushed down into the primary grades, teachers feel the need to spend time on academic content, rather than allowing children opportunities to build language.

Woodward et al (2004) mentioned that teachers in Buffalo, New York, were concerned over finding a two-year deficit in language among their kindergarten children. Knowing that oral language is a predictor in the literacy development of children, the teachers implemented "table talk" in their preschool and kindergarten urban classrooms. After participating in professional development regarding the development of oral language, the teachers introduced the "Let's Talk" approach to facilitate children's interactions. Using the Brigance screening test to identify children with low language skills, these children were paired with classmates who had higher language skills for 15 minutes per day. The role of each teacher was to manage the centers, which comprised boxes of carefully selected dramatic play toys, and stimulate conversation, if needed. Pre- and posttest results showed positive improvements across such survey factors as vocabulary, comprehension, information, main idea, and gesturing. Several factors seemed to contribute to the success of the Let's Talk approach to oral language development:

* Children worked together in designated pairs at the tables, with little intervention from adults.
* Manipulatives used for the table talks were rotated weekly to initiate new conversations.
* Teachers modeled literature and vocabulary related to the manipulatives each week.
* Opportunities for sharing with others were provided routinely in the classroom.
* Extensions related to the manipulatives were integrated throughout the curriculum.

This article brings a fresh perspective to dramatic play in early childhood classrooms. Teachers will find the table talk approach in this article easy to implement in their classrooms.

Theory and strategy were combined to examine the potential benefits for children who find reading to be a challenge. The theoretical foundation of culturally responsive teaching was used to include children's language and background when facilitating literacy connections. Culturally responsive teaching, as posited by Neuman (1999), affects curriculum through: 1) recognition and value of the child's culture, 2) promotion of collaboration, 3) establishment of high standards and expectations of all children, and 4) appreciation of the importance of continuity between literacy found in the home and in the school.

The strategy, Text Talk (Beck & McKeown, 2001), typically used with emergent readers, uses challenging texts to develop oral language and comprehension through focused read alouds. Texts are carefully selected to represent topics that are relevant to the child's world. The authors combined Text Talk with culturally responsive teaching to facilitate the potential for engagement with challenging content language and ideas (Conrad, et al. 2004). As practitioners, we must continue to look for innovative, more culturally sensitive ways to connect school with children's life experiences. Culturally responsive teaching through Text Talk provides an option to bridge this gap, opening the door for more opportunities for the development of oral language and comprehension in the pursuit of literacy.

Effective inclusive early childhood education classrooms focus on the role of language development in literacy. Even though many assessments used in early childhood classrooms evaluate language development, there is little evidence that these assessments are being used to drive instruction. In fact, Rowell (1998) found that only 10 percent of 67 preschool classes observed used purposeful instruction with vocabulary. Historically, many teachers have taken a more incidental approach to language development, resulting in greater literacy deficits by grade 3. The author of this article recommends embedded learning opportunities (ELO) to enhance the potential for language learning through purposeful experiences. The specific techniques used in ELO are self-talk, parallel talk, expansion, and elaboration. These techniques are infused into the learning centers of the classroom, with a target on specific vocabulary related to the experiences in the centers.

The author examined the children's language development in a quantitative and qualitative manner. Quantitative language, or the number of words a child uses, is an important predictor of literacy success. Research suggests that teachers could use targeted questions to promote the development of new language by the children who begin school with a deficit in language. In planning particular centers or activities, teachers can consider the type of vocabulary stimulated by the activity and the vocabulary children might need to interact with others appropriately during the activity. Additionally, the teacher should look at connections that could be made with the functional activities of the home and school. Finally, teachers can think about the academic and social vocabulary the child would need in the future. Even children who come to school with a large vocabulary need to have their vocabulary enhanced continually.

Qualitative language development, as represented through in-depth usage in multiple contexts, focuses on the nouns, verbs, adjectives, etc., needed in a particular area of the room. The dramatic play area is an example of a context where children use language that is familiar both at home and in school. The hope is that rich language experiences can help children begin to use more sophisticated ways of speaking in all contexts

Additionally, the cognitively challenging conversations that occur at critical times during the preschool day provide opportunities for teachers and caregivers to model and promote oral language and literacy development. These conversations engage children in conversations that involve explanations, personal narrative, and pretend play where children create and re-create events, analyze experiences, and share opinions and ideas. This is different from the traditional talk found in many classrooms, which typically is centered around procedural or management information.

Massey provides ways to incorporate the four levels of abstract language into classroom interactions. Moving from a low form of complexity, such as labeling objects, to higher level skills of reasoning related to making predictions, solving problems, and explaining concepts, children develop discourse along a continuum of complexities. These levels of language development are best incorporated through the contexts of book reading, playtime, and mealtimes.

The author encourages teachers to thoughtfully plan for rich talk related to book readings, recommending 45 minutes per day for reading aloud. The talk used should be both immediate, relating to the actual reading experience, and non-immediate, using the illustrations of books to initiate high-level questioning. Rereading provides natural venues for these conversations. Dialogic reading allows children to retell the story (including their personal elaborations), thereby building oral language skills and, ultimately, literacy skills.

Teachers should also make themselves available to interact with children during playtime. A teacher who is stationary in the classroom is more likely to engage children in cognitively challenging conversations than one who is circulating around the room. Teachers also can promote pretend talk by modeling or providing props to retell stories. This pretend talk encourages children to make connections between their play in the classroom and at their homes. Meal/snack times are also good opportunities to introduce unfamiliar vocabulary within a relevant context. As we listen to the topics that children are conversing about, we can interject vocabulary or elaborate on children's conversations.

Massey promotes a targeted planning of rich conversation opportunities in preschool classrooms. She states that a focus on talk during the day seems to have a greater impact as a predictor of literacy success for young children than does the classroom environment. Infants and toddlers first attempt to communicate through gestures. They express their emotional and physical needs through such gestures as holding out their arms to be picked up and tugging on adults' hair or pointing to objects in an attempt to get adults' attention. The response of adults to children's gesturing affects children's development of verbal communication. Honig explains that seemingly simple activities that encourage children's gesturing, such as finger-plays, are important interactions between adults and babies. Adults should label the objects children need to identify to encourage association between objects and language. Modeling appropriate gestures ensures that children begin to build on interactions that will aid their social development.

Through gesturing, the toddlers' communicative world expands. Large motor games, such as ring-around-the-rosie, encourage talk among peers. Toddlers also can enjoy copycat gestures. The important point to remember is that any gesture activities planned for toddlers should be appropriate for their age and development. A letter for parents is included in the article to promote understanding and patience with babies and toddlers as they make sense of the world. Teachers can use the letter as a model to educate parents in their classrooms about this important part of a child's language development.

As we take a comprehensive examination of children's language development and the roles that adults play in that journey, we discover that the variety of language used at home and school has a direct bearing on children's literacy. Based on the complexity of the language development processes, caregivers in the home and school need to be aware of ways to enhance opportunities for children to learn effective communication. In school, teachers facilitate language development opportunities through environments that provide safety and security so that children feel enabled to explore with language. Children feel valued when their expressions are acknowledged in a respectful manner. Teachers can enhance the development of language by elaborating on children's stories, rather than correcting them. The diversity of languages and dialects brought to the classroom by children and teachers enhances such opportunities. Seefeldt includes ideas for teachers to use when working with children who are English language learners.

A well-planned environment provides children access to materials needed for exploration and talk with peers about their ideas. Within these social interactions, children negotiate their understandings of the world and their role in it. In this article, the reader can find examples of appropriate materials for centers in the classroom that enhance children's language development. When teachers plan centers around a common topic, children are more likely to make connections with their world and construct associated language.

The teacher's role in the classroom is to model language, elaborating on children's expressions when appropriate. Validation of children's ideas encourages them to become risk takers as they navigate the schooling process. Acknowledging both the positive and negative emotions of children helps them to develop the language they need when interacting with peers. This provides a foundation for compromise and negotiation as children mature. Even seemingly insignificant nonverbal signals, changes in voice tones, and facial expressions cue children about appropriate social interactions.

The role of parents in children's literacy development is critical. Quality early childhood programs recognize the importance of educating parents so they can scaffold their children's literacy development in the home. Strickland emphasizes the interrelatedness of oral language and literacy and the role parents play in facilitating that process.

Children's early knowledge about speaking and listening contributes to the development of their reading and writing. Since language and literacy develop together, parents can engage children in chants, songs, and rhymes to facilitate the phonological awareness needed for success with early reading skills. If this language and literacy development is impeded, school achievement lags, initially and throughout the primary grades. Additionally, the experiences parents provide for children should be contextual in nature, rather than provided in isolation. Typically, parents need to be informed about this point; as they perform the everyday functional literacy tasks, they also can provide the modeling needed to facilitate language development.

Language develops differently for children who come from homes that are language-poor. Hart and Risely (1995) found that not only are these children exposed to different kinds of words in their homes, but the words are fewer in number and typically used in a more punitive manner. Therefore, the amount of vocabulary a child constructs is greatly affected by this lack of discourse in the home. Consequently, Strickland provides key implications for parents and educators to recognize in order to provide quality experiences for children in oral language and print activities.

Have we put the proverbial "cart before the horse" with regard to content standards for preschoolers? As part of the Distinguished Educator series on "The Role of Literacy in Early Childhood Education," Schickedanz suggests that the content standards for preschools should reflect our knowledge of the research related to language and literacy development. With the pressure placed on schools to meet specific benchmarks with the No Child Left Behind legislation, educators are becoming more concerned about what our preschools are teaching. The results of this concern have been an overemphasis on literacy skills and a lack of emphasis on oral language skills. Schickedanz warns that such a view of literacy learning will not serve children well. Although some educators believe that oral language does not directly affect literacy skills (Snow, 2002; Storch & Whitehurst, 2002), poor language skills do tend to affect reading achievement in the primary years (Hart & Risley, 1995).

In consideration of this shift in thinking, the author proposes a more balanced look at content standards for preschools that would include language and literacy. The article concludes with a proposed example of pre-kindergarten content standards that states could consider. Administrators will find this table very helpful in redefining and evaluating the content of preschool and early childhood curriculums.

When and How Language is Learned

Almost all children learn the rules of their language at an early age through use, and over time, without formal instruction. Thus one source for learning must be genetic. Human beings are born to speak; they have an innate gift for figuring out the rules of the language used in their environment. The environment itself is also a significant factor. Children learn the specific variety of language (dialect) that the important people around them speak.

Children do not, however, learn only by imitating those around them. We know that children work through linguistic rules on their own because they use forms that adults never use, such as "I goed there before" or "I see your feets." Children eventually learn the conventional forms, "went" and "feet", as they sort out for themselves the exceptions to the rules of English syntax. As with learning to walk, learning to talk requires time for development and practice in everyday situations. Constant correction of a child's speech is usually unproductive.

Children seem born not just to speak, but also to interact socially. Even before they use words, they use cries and gestures to convey meaning; they often understand the meanings that others convey. The point of learning language and interacting socially, then, is not to master rules, but to make connections with other people and to make sense of experiences (Wells, 1986). In summary, language occurs through an interaction among genes (which hold innate tendencies to communicate and be sociable), environment, and the child's own thinking abilities.

When children develop abilities is always a difficult question to answer. In general, children say their first words between 12 and 18 months of age. They begin to use complex sentences by the age of 4 to 4 1/2 years. By the time they start kindergarten, children know most of the fundamentals of their language, so that they are able to converse easily with someone who speaks as they do (that is, in their dialect). As with other aspects of development, language acquisition is not predictable. One child may say her first word at 10 months, another at 20 months. One child may use complex sentences at 5 1/2 years, another at 3 years

Oral Language Components

Oral language, the complex system that relates sounds to meanings, is made up of three components: the phonological, semantic, and syntactic (Lindfors, 1987). The phonological component involves the rules for combining sounds. Speakers of English, for example, know that an English word can end, but not begin, with an "-ng" sound. We are not aware of our knowledge of these rules, but our ability to understand and pronounce English words demonstrates that we do know a vast number of rules.

The semantic component is made up of morphemes, the smallest units of meaning that may be combined with each other to make up words (for example, "paper" + "s" are the two morphemes that make up "papers"), and sentences (Brown, 1973). A dictionary contains the semantic component of a language, and reflects not just what words make up that language, but also what words (and meanings) are important to the speakers of the language.

The syntactic component consists of the rules that enable us to combine morphemes into sentences. As soon as a child uses two morphemes together, as in "more cracker," she is using a syntactic rule about how morphemes are combined to convey meaning. Like the rules making up the other components, syntactic rules become increasingly complex as the child develops. From combining two morphemes, the child goes on to combine words with suffixes or inflections ("-s" or "-ing", as in "papers" and "eating") and eventually creates questions, statements, commands, etc. She also learns to combine two ideas into one complex sentence, as in "I'll share my crackers if you share your juice." Of course speakers of a language constantly use these three components of language together, usually in social situations.

Some language experts would add a fourth component: pragmatics, which deals with rules of language use. Pragmatic rules are part of our communicative competence, our ability to speak appropriately in different situations, for example, in a conversational way at home and in a more formal way at a job interview. Young children need to learn the ways of speaking in the day care center or school where, for example, teachers often ask rhetorical questions. Learning pragmatic rules is as important as learning the rules of the other components of language since people are perceived and judged based on both what they say and how and when they say it.

Nurturing Language Development

Parents and caregivers need to remember that language in the great majority of individuals develops very efficiently. Adults should try not to focus on "problems," such as the inability to pronounce words as adults do (for example, when children pronounce r's like w's). Most children naturally outgrow such things, which are a tiny segment of the child's total repertoire of language. However, if a child appears not to hear what others say to her; if family members and those closest to her find her difficult to understand; or if she is noticeably different in her communicative abilities from those in her age range, adults may want to seek advice from specialists in children's speech, language and hearing.

* Teachers can help sustain natural language development by providing environments full of language development opportunities. Here are some general guidelines for teachers, parents, and other caregivers:
* Understand that every child's language or dialect is worthy of respect as a valid system for communication. It reflects the identities, values, and experiences of the child's family and community.

* Treat children as if they are conversationalists, even if they are not yet talking. Children learn very early about how conversations work (taking turns, looking attentively, using facial expressions, etc.) as long as they have experiences with conversing adults.
* Encourage interaction among children. Peer learning is an important part of language development, especially in mixed-age groups. Activities involving a wide range of materials should promote talk. There should be a balance between individual activities and those that nurture collaboration and discussion, such as dramatic play, block-building, book-sharing, or carpentry.

Remember that parents, caregivers, teachers, and guardians are the chief resources in language development. Children learn much from each other, but adults are the main conversationalists, questioners, listeners, responders, and sustainers of language development and growth in the child-care center or classroom. Continue to encourage interaction as children come to understand written language. Children in the primary grades can keep developing oral abilities and skills by consulting with each other, raising questions, and providing information in varied situations. Every area of the curriculum is enhanced through language, so that classrooms full of active learners are hardly ever silent.

Oral Language Development across the Curriculum

At the most basic level, oral language means communicating with other people. But when we talk about oral language development across the curriculum, we do not mean teaching children to speak as much as we mean improving their ability to talk or communicate more effectively. Speech is not usually simply basic communication--it involves thinking, knowledge, and skills. It also requires practice and training. How can we help our children to develop oral proficiency? What do we need to do as teachers to facilitate that development? These are the questions we will discuss in this Digest.

Oral language acquisition is a natural process for children. It occurs almost without effort. The ability to speak grows with age, but it does not mean that such growth will automatically lead to perfection. To speak in more effective ways requires particular attention and constant practice. Holbrook (1983) sets out three criteria for oral language competence: fluency, clarity, and sensitivity. To help children achieve these levels of development is our responsibility as educators.

Teacher Role

Many studies have indicated that oral language development has largely been neglected in the classroom (Holbrook, 1983). Most of the time oral language in the classroom is used more by teachers than by students. However, oral language, even as used by the teacher, seldom functions as a means for students to gain knowledge and to explore ideas.

Underlying this fact are two assumptions. One of these assumptions--that the teacher's role is to teach--is usually interpreted to mean that to teach means to talk. Accordingly, teachers spend hours and hours teaching by talking while the children sit listening passively. Such conventional teaching-learning is one of the obstacles preventing the real development of oral language. Children leaving these classrooms tend to carry this passivity over to their learning attitudes, and tend to be "disabled" in their learning abilities, as well.

The second assumption is based on the fact that children start learning and using oral language long before they go to school. Therefore, it is assumed that the primary learning tasks for children in school are reading and writing, which are usually seen as the two major aspects of literacy. In one investigation Stabb (1986) reported a steady decline of the use of oral language in classrooms as a major reason for the inhibition of students' abilities to reason and to forecast as they progressed from lower to higher grades. Such a phenomenon is found not only in the language arts classroom, but also in other classrooms. According to Stabb's and many other researchers' observations, classrooms are dominated by teachers talking and by workbook exercises. Researchers call this phenomenon "teachers-talk-students-listen" or "teacher-dominated." In related research, Willmington (1993) surveyed school administrators who attested to the importance of oral communication skills for teachers--and they considered listening to be the most important skill of all.

Another result of teacher-dominated classrooms is the negative effect upon children's attitudes toward learning. Operating under the two above-mentioned assumptions, teachers often fail to see that literacy learning is a continuum, an ongoing process of learning, for children. Learning before going to school and learning in school are often viewed as separate processes. Oral language, which is the major learning instrument for children before going to school, is no longer available with the onset of formal schooling. Confronted with new tasks of learning to read and write while being deprived of their major learning tool, children tend to feel depressed and frustrated. Learning begins to loom large, and schooling gradually becomes routine, exactly the situation described in Stabb's research.

After a few years students will have become programmed to a kind of passive learning atmosphere, the teacher talks, the students listen and do their homework. Here, learning simply means taking down whatever is given. In this type of classroom environment, students learn the basic skills of reading and writing. However, they will not learn how to think critically and how to make sound judgments on their own. Stabb (1986) speculates that we teachers often become "so involved with establishing routine, finishing the textbook, covering curriculum, and preparing students for standardized tests that we have forgotten one of our original goals, that of stimulating thought." Though Stabb's speculation sounds critical, she does provide us with a thought-provoking expansion of the relationship between oral language development and thinking abilities development. In delineating a debate program for elementary school students, Aiex (1990) notes that, although the focus of the program is on the development of oral communication skills, critical thinking and reasoning abilities are also developed along the way.

Oral language as foundation

From the preceding, we can see that oral language is indeed an important link in the process of children's learning and thinking development. It is not merely a language issue; it is also an intellectual issue which deserves serious attention from both teachers and researchers. From the perspective of language development, oral language provides a foundation for the development of other language skills. For most children, the literacy learning process actually begins with speaking, talking about their experiences, talking about themselves. It is through speech that children learn to organize their thinking and focus their ideas (Lyle, 1993). The neglect of oral language in the classroom will destroy that foundation and severely hinder the development of other aspects of language skills.

Research on cognitive development

Current research literature on critical thinking and cognitive development indicates that the development of language has a close relationship to the development of thinking abilities (Berry, 1985; Gambell, 1988). This is especially true for elementary-level students. Before achieving proficiency in reading and writing--and even after proficiency in reading and writing have been achieved--oral language is one of the important means of learning and of acquiring knowledge (Lemke, 1989). Throughout life, oral language skills remain essential for engagement in intellectual dialogue, and for the communication of ideas.

Teacher as facilitator

Given this understanding of the importance of oral language skills, we should reflect on our attitudes toward the teaching-learning relationship. First of all, we need to overcome the faulty assumptions mentioned before. As teachers, we should not assume the role of authoritarian knowledge giver. Instead, we should see ourselves as friendly and interested facilitators of student learning. In emphasizing the role of oral language in the classroom, we are by no means implying that the teacher's role is not important; on the contrary, we present a more demanding task for teachers. To facilitate a learning process in which children are given both opportunity and encouragement to speak and to explore their own thinking, the teacher has to do more than tell children what he or she means, or what the text means. Instead, the teacher has several different roles to play.

The teacher can encourage students to bring their ideas and background knowledge into class learning activities. To achieve this goal, the teacher must be a good and responsive listener to children's talk. Facilitation of a child's talking in class is not enough for language teaching, however, but only provides an environment conducive to both teaching and learning. At this point, the teacher can raise questions concerning the content of the class or the text. While maintaining the role of a knowing arbiter, the teacher still needs to persuade the students. Here one point should be emphasized--implementation of oral language development across the curriculum requires teamwork. All content-area teachers have to be actively involved in this task. The goal is not only to get children to speak, but also to have them learn and develop through speech.

As the children's other language skills develop in the course of time, classroom talk can be directed more towards the goals of exploring ideas found in texts and sharpening thoughts. "Speaking to learn" is the vehicle for increasing and deepening knowledge. Two publications recommended as resource guides for classroom teachers are "Guidelines for Developing Oral Communication Curricula in Kindergarten through Twelfth Grade" and "Listening and Speaking in the English Language Arts Curricula K-12

Teachers can help sustain natural language development by providing environments full of language development opportunities. Here is a general guideline for teachers, parents, and other caregivers:

- Understand that every child's language or dialect is worthy of respect as a valid system for language use.

Pragmatic rules are part of our communicative competence, our ability to speak appropriately in different situations, for example, in a conversational way at home and in a more formal way at a job interview. Young children need to learn the ways of speaking in the day care center or school where, for example, teachers often ask rhetorical questions. Learning pragmatic rules is as important as learning the rules of the other components of language since people are perceived and judged based on both what they say and how and when they say it.

Chapter II

Print Concepts

It is very important for children to start pre-literacy activities at an early age. These activities will help children develop concepts about print. These concepts include knowing how to hold a book the right way, differentiating between print and pictures, turning pages left to right, and being able to tell the front of the book from the back (Ornstein, 1998). Once children have grasped these first basic concepts, children can move on to learning more complex concepts about text. Children will learn that one must read lines of text from left to right and then to go back to the beginning of the next line down. They will also learn that pages are read from top to bottom starting at the top left. Next children will learn to tell words from letters, "two different letters, a capital and a lowercase letter, and two different words" (Ornstein, 1998, p. 60). Lastly they will pick up on punctuation marks in texts. Each of these stages of gaining concepts can be aided by parents and family members with different kinds of books that I will discuss later.

Developing concepts about print in children at an early age is invaluable to their literacy development. Without a firm grasp on these concepts, children will have trouble learning to read and write. These concepts about text give children the tools they need to read and to write by themselves. In addition, children's knowledge of these concepts when they enter kindergarten is a major factor in determining their literacy level (Nichols, Rupley, & Rickleman, 2004). Developing these concepts through early literacy experiences is so important that both the National Association for the Education of Young Children and the International Reading Association state that "failing to give children literacy experiences until they are of school-age can severely limit the reading and writing levels they ultimately attain" (Rog, 2001, p. 10).

Families can help children develop these concepts about print by exposing them to books, magazines, and all kinds of print, especially in their homes. Having a variety of texts at home helps children learn about how text works. Lack of exposure to text may limit children's ability to develop an understanding of these concepts. Children exposed to books and other reading material at a young age will begin to try to imitate writing and reading if given the opportunity (Rog, 2001).

Families can help their children develop these important concepts about texts in many simple ways. Reading to your children and reading in the presence of your children are both easy ways to help them with these concepts. You can begin reading to your children even before they begin to talk (Campbell, 1998). The first books you may want to try reading should have many pictures and not that many words per page with large print. You might also want to use board books so that your children do not tear the pages (Ornstein, 1998). A book such as *Pat the Bunny* by Dorothy Kunhardt would be an excellent book for gaining the first concepts of reading. As you read with your children, ask them questions (Campbell, 1998) and talk about the book. Also, allow your children to turn the pages of the book and hold the book if they can or want to do so.

After having experience with board books and learning how to hold a book and turn its pages, children will start to focus on the text more. Identify the title of the book, and ask your children to predict what the book is going to be about by looking at the cover. Ask them to show you what part of the page you should begin reading (the text versus the picture). When you read to your children, you might begin to guide their fingers across the words as you read pointing to each word as you say it. This will help them see that for each word you say there is a set of letters on the paper that corresponds; this is called one-to-one matching (Ornstein, 1998). Once you have read a short book to your children several times, ask them to try reading it to you, having your children re-tell the story in their own words (Miller, 1995). In this stage of development, you should pick books with large print and few lines per page with a good amount of space between the words (Ornstein, 1998). A good book for this level is *Where the Wild Things Are* by Maurice Sendak. This book also has lively and interesting pictures that children will enjoy.

Next as children begin to notice the difference between a letter and a word, they will need families to read them a new level of books. They might enjoy some rhyming books such as the Dr. Seuss books, *Cat in the Hat* and *Hop on Pop* (Ornstein, 1998). Lastly, as children begin to read more fluently, they will enjoy books that have to do specifically with things of interest to them. The stories in the *Mrs. Piggle Wiggle* series may be popular at this stage though children will still need guidance from family members on these stories.

Family Activities

- Bring your children to the grocery store with you. Before going, have them help you dictate the grocery list to you and watch you as you write the words. Say the words out loud as you write them. When you get to the grocery store, read your list out-loud as you point to the words and point to the corresponding words on the products you are buying. This activity will help children understand the practical use of print in action. They will see that you write left to right just like you read left to right also.
- Make a book with your children. Very young children might like a book of familiar photographs with labels under each photo that a family member can read to him or her. Older children might like to illustrate the book by themselves. You could write the words as the children dictate the story. Then you and your children could read the book together, pointing to the words as you read.

- Take your children to a restaurant. Show them the menu and whatever pictures may be on the menu. Read the menu to your children pointing to the words as you do. Let them help choose what to eat and have them point to it if they can remember which one it is. This activity will also help children realize how we use print in real life.
- Read to your children! The number one thing you can do for your children to help them learn print concepts is to read to them everyday. A bedtime story is an excellent opportunity to read to your children. Make sure the book is interesting to your children. Ask them to predict what will happen in the book and guide their fingers along the words.

Elements of Classroom Environment

Physical Space

Physical space refers to the arrangement of the classroom (furniture and wall space) and the organization of materials that support literacy and encourage independence in students. The classroom arrangement can encourage varied encounters with print and facilitate large and small group conversations (in a library area, comfortable reading spaces, meeting area with easel, or literacy centers). The wall space can display attractive, organized, environmental print that reflects students' lives and backgrounds. Placing students' artwork and writing on the walls give students ownership in their classroom. Reading and writing materials can be arranged to be inviting and accessible.

Materials and Tools

Materials and tools are the objects and print materials used to engage students in literacy activities. Examples include the following: word walls that foster word recognition and correct spelling; an attendance chart that builds name recognition and initial letter identification; work boards or job charts that allow students to move independently through tasks; enlarged poetry or other charts that model reading strategies and encourage independent practice; pointers for reading that help students attend to and build concepts about print; and stamp pads and letter cubes that help students practice building words.

Techniques and Management Practices

Classroom routines, organizational techniques, and management practices can establish a productive learning environment that promotes literacy while also encouraging student independence and community responsibility. Examples include daily attendance using a pocket chart with students' names to encourage responsibility for checking in while building name recognition and letter awareness; daily morning meetings that provide opportunities for language development and for specific instruction in reading and writing; classroom jobs; and opportunities for student leadership of daily routines.

Tone and Atmosphere

The tone and atmosphere of a classroom are conveyed through the teacher's voice, word choice, body language, and physical positioning, as well as through the arrangement of the room and organization of classroom routines. The tone and atmosphere can communicate the following: the belief that all students can learn and are capable of taking responsibility; enthusiasm for all forms of literacy; the clear purpose of each instructional activity; a clarity of expectations; an appreciation of individual differences; and responsiveness and flexibility. A teacher sitting next to the students on the floor or helping shy students communicate their work through drawings are situations that create such an inclusive atmosphere

Directionality

Directionality refers to the way print is tracked during reading and laid down during writing. Children must know to begin at the top of the page and work toward the bottom, starting on the left-hand side and moving to the right.

Young children must also learn how to move from the end of one line of print to the beginning of the next using a "return sweep." This movement essentially means that when going on to a new line of text, the child returns to the left-hand side of the paper and works across the page again.

Children develop directionality gradually during the emergent period and during the transition into conventional literacy. Fluctuations during early years usually are not a reason for concern.

Word-by-Word Matching

Word-by-word matching is the ability to match words printed on a page to spoken words. This concept applies to both reading and writing tasks as children gradually learn to relate spoken words to written words. Word-by-word matching is not the same as recognizing words on sight. Sight-word recognition is the ability to see a word and know automatically what the word is.

Children who perform word-by-word matching while writing, create (through either invented or conventional spelling) complete messages on paper with proper spacing between words. The child understands that what is spoken also can be written down. This matching emerges gradually, and the child's control often fluctuates

Reading Comprehension: The Components of Reading

Concepts of print refers to all the concepts related to how print is organized and used in reading and writing tasks. Several concepts must be attended to by young learners: letter vs. word, first and last, directionality, and word-by-word matching. Children understand the concept of letter vs. word when they recognize a difference between letters and words and realize that words are composed of letters. Children also must develop an understanding of "first and last" as it relates to words, sentences, and whole texts.

As mentioned before, **concepts about print** include awareness that: print carries a message. Additionally, there are conventions of print such as directionality (left to right, top to bottom), differences between letters and words, distinctions between upper and lower case, punctuation; and books have some common characteristics (e.g. author, title, front/back). Classroom practices that support the acquisition of concepts of print for emergent readers include: Have class helpers search for distinguishing features of the **front** of books as they clean up the class library and arrange them properly in book display racks.

- Model **directionality** and **one to one matching** by pointing to words while using enlarged text in a big book, pocket chart, poem or song chart. With repeated readings the language of the text is learned and the children can practice following along or eventually match the words they say with the print on the page independently. They may practice by pointing to words with their finger or any number of homemade pointers (chopsticks, dowels with pom poms on the ends, rubber witchy fingers, etc.)
- Leave multiple pieces of familiar text (songs, poems, rhymes, etc.) posted in the room at a child's eye level to be available for students to "read around the room" independently.
- Write a brief, familiar rhyme or poem on individual word cards and assemble them on a pocket chart. Construct and reconstruct the text on the pocket chart with the children developing an awareness of directionality, one to one matching of the print to spoken words, spacing conventions, punctuation, etc.
- Have children search familiar text to locate an upper or lowercase letter, a known word, punctuation, etc. Highlighting tape, sticky notes, wikki sticks and children's fingers can be used to isolate and locate a variety of conventions of print in a piece of familiar text.
- Use interactive writing to provide opportunities for constructing text with children. Model, share and support the writing task for emergent writers. As the teacher "thinks aloud" throughout the task children have the opportunity to hear about a variety of print concepts and practice using them. (e.g. Should we put our first word at the top or the bottom? Will the first letter go on the right or the left? Should the **M** in Mark be upper or lowercase? What goes at the end of our sentence?)

- Use magnetic letters, word titles or even name cards to complete sorts emphasizing similarities and differences between words and letters. (e.g. Put all the uppercase letters in this pile. Find all the words that have the letter B.)
- Create a pocket chart activity using a few known sight words, children's name cards and periods, exclamation marks and question marks. Practice reading simple sentences like the examples below. Students can develop an understanding of the importance of punctuation as it alters the reading of such simply constructed texts as:

  Mary can jump.

  I can run!

  Can Paul sing?

* Print carries a message. Even when a child "play reads" text using pictures and memory, the child demonstrates an understanding of this concept, even if she cannot read the words, or reads them backwards or front to back.
- Books are organized, with a cover, title, and author, and reading in English flows in a particular and consistent direction, left to right and top to bottom. When young students successfully point to or otherwise track the print as someone reads aloud, they demonstrate their understanding of orientation and directionality.
- Printed language consists of letters, words, and sentences. The emergent reader gradually learns to distinguish between these forms, learns the concepts of "beginning" and "end," and understands punctuation that marks text (e.g., period, comma, and question mark).
- Recognition of matching or upper- and lower-case letters, as well as some common spelling sequences, is slightly more complex concepts of print mastered by more experienced beginning readers.

Additionally, concepts about print can be taught using shared reading of Big Books, enlarged charts and poems, or other kinds of engaging texts. It can also be taught through interactive writing, language experience dictations, or exploring print in the classroom environment. Many teachers use Clay's Concepts about Print assessment tool in late kindergarten or beginning first grade to assess students' concepts about print.

CUING STRATEGIES

Used by effective readers to figure out unfamiliar words and to make meaning, cuing strategies include knowledge of syntax, semantics, words and word meaning, and graphophonics (letter/sound associations).

Teachers can guide students to use cuing strategies by reminding them to ask themselves, "Did it sound right? Did it make sense? Did the word look right?"

English Language Learner

An English language learner (ELL) is a student who speaks one or more languages other than English and who is just developing proficiency in English. In this video library, both dual language learning and careful scaffolding of literacy experiences in English enhance ELL students' learning of oral and written English.

Invented (or Temporary) Spelling

A child's attempt at spelling a word using what they know about the English spelling system is referred to as invented or temporary spelling. Invented spelling allows emergent writers to explore written language and experiment with writing at a very early stage. Early writing is a valuable developmental indicator of the conventional spelling patterns and the sound/symbol relationships the child has internalized. It can be used to help the teacher's instruction. (Literacy Dictionary, p. 128)

Metacognition

Metacognition is the awareness individuals have of their own mental processes and the subsequent ability to monitor, regulate, and direct themselves to a desired end. A student demonstrates metacognition if she can articulate what strategies she used to read and understand a text. Metacognition helps readers monitor and control their comprehension on an ongoing basis and adjust their reading strategies to maximize comprehension. (The *Literacy Dictionary*, p. 128)

Miscue

Based on Goodman's findings in the mid-1960s, a miscue is any departure from the text when reading orally. Use of miscue instead of "error" suggests that mistakes are not random, but occur when the reader tries to use different strategies to make sense of text, and emphasizes that not all errors are equal, some errors represent more highly developed reading skills than others. Miscues can be analyzed to suggest what strategies the reader is using or lacking, and what kinds of additional instruction might be helpful. (Harris & Hodge, (1995)

Miscue Analysis

Miscue analysis is a way of closely observing, recording, and analyzing oral reading behaviors to assess how the reader is using specific cuing strategies, like the use of syntax, semantic information, and graphophonics. The teacher uses a specific code to record actual reading. Miscue analysis is usually done with an unfamiliar, long text, followed by a taped retelling. Scoring and analysis is more complex than with a running record, and is usually done at a later time. While running records are most often used with beginning readers, miscue analysis can be used for more advanced readers.

Onset and Rime

Most words and many syllables can be separated into onsets (the initial consonant sound such as /c/ in cat) and rimes or phonograms (the vowel and letters which follow, such as /-at/). Whole words can be separated into onsets and rimes, such as "/f/ /-or/," as can syllables, such as /"tr/ /-ans/ /f/ /-orm/. Some words and syllables have only rimes, such as "/on/" or "/-ing/".

Print-Rich Environment

A print-rich environment refers to classroom displays of written language -- both teacher-made, student-generated, and published materials -- like books, charts, students' work journals, and stories. A print rich-environment helps students acquire concepts about print as they learn how print is used. Students can "read around the room." For example, the calendar, lunch menu, list of classroom jobs, or the morning message all emphasize that print carries meaning. Students can refer to print displays to help their reading and spelling. (Ready for RICA, pp. 27-28)

Running Record

A running record (RR) is a method for closely observing and assessing a student's oral reading of a complete story or book, or 150-300 words excerpted from a longer text. Running records can be taken spontaneously on the fly without advance preparation, using whatever text the student happens to be reading; or they can be taken using a photocopy of a prepared text. Running records differ from miscue analysis because they are simpler to use on a day-to-day basis in the classroom.

Running records can be used to assess familiar text for accuracy and fluency. Or they may be used with new texts to see how the student applies reading strategies. Running records may be taken weekly or monthly to document growth over time, or periodically (two or three times a year) as part of an assessment profile to place students in reading groups or to document progress along specific benchmarks.

To take a running record, the teacher sits close enough to see the text as the student reads aloud and uses a special code to mark the precise reading response. Without comment, the teacher marks a check for each word read accurately and notes any substitutions, omissions, additions, and self-corrections. This process usually takes about 10 minutes, but it may take less time with an emergent reader.

At the end of the reading, the teacher quickly totals the number of miscues and self-corrections, and then calculates the rate of reading accuracy and self-correction. The calculation helps the teacher determine whether reading material is at an appropriate level and what subsequent texts might be chosen. The teacher can also analyze the types of miscues made on the RR to understand what reading strategies the child uses and what kinds of additional instruction might be helpful.

SELF-MONITOR

Students self-monitor when they pay attention to their own work to make sure that it is clear and makes sense. During reading, students attend to meaning and use fix-up strategies such as re-reading or reading ahead to clarify meaning. During writing, students check and reflect on the clarity of the message and on the features of text (words, grammar, and conventions) they need to communicate effectively with an audience. In this video library, students self-monitor during interactive writing when they discuss and analyze their writing and during independent writing when they check for meaning and grammar. Students also self-monitor during shared and guided reading when they think aloud to share their understanding of a text with the teacher or with other students. Self-monitoring is an aspect of metacognition. (The Literacy Dictionary, p. 229)

WORD WALLS

A word wall is made up of carefully selected and displayed lists or groups of words used by students to build familiarity with common sight words. They serve as visual scaffolds, provide students with familiar word patterns to assist them in decoding unfamiliar words, and are useful when students write. Word walls do the following:

- build word recognition;
- facilitate word analysis;
- serve as a reference for commonly misspelled words; and
- build vocabulary for a new text or content area.

Word walls are used by students and teachers to see and monitor what has been taught and learned. They are used for planned instruction and as a resource for unplanned instructional opportunities, or "teachable moments," that arise unexpectedly during the day. (Brabham & Villaume. (2001), "Building Walls of Words.

Yvonne L. Simon

Although phonological awareness is important for early reading comprehension, other skills become important as students develop their reading abilities. Designed to facilitate successful early reading for kindergarten students, this lesson teaches the acquisition of vocabulary, one-to-one matching, left-to-right directionality, and awareness of rhyme. Students study these important aspects of reading using a shared exploration of a poem that includes peer interaction, hands-on experience with print, and a collaborative examination of new and familiar words (Gambrell, 2004).

Studies show that although phonological awareness is critically important to word decoding, other language skills may become more influential as students learn to read. In fact, whether or not students can find meaning in printed words and their awareness of the print around them are greater predictors of reading comprehension in the first and second grades than phonological awareness. Vocabulary knowledge and print awareness are important factors in reading ability, both at the individual word level and for overall comprehension. The author encourages educators to use the following plan as a guide to their instruction.

* Learn about important concepts of print including left-to-right directionality and one-to-one matching by talking about where they should begin reading a poem and watching spoken words matched to print during read-alouds of the poem.
* Demonstrate word recognition critical to reading comprehension by matching words to print as they are being read and by identifying familiar words in a poem
* Demonstrate understanding of rhyming words by identifying and discussing them in a nursery rhyme and creating a list of words that rhyme with key rhyming words from the text.
* Practice acquiring and using new vocabulary by identifying an unfamiliar word, discussing it, and using it to create a predictable class book.

Resources

Row, Row, Row Your Boat

- Flip Book
- "Kittens"
- Chart paper
- Computers with Internet access
- Highlight tape
- Highlighters
- Pointer
- White board with marker

Reading Comprehension: The Components of Reading

Instructional Plan

Preparation

1. It is important to break these activities into six sessions as shown in the Instruction and Activities. Designate a comfortable meeting area in the classroom that will seat all students for group work.
2. Write the nursery rhyme "Kittens" (or another nursery rhyme you have chosen to use with your class) on a piece of chart paper so that all students will be able to see it. The poem you choose should have at least one unfamiliar word in it. (You might also choose "I Had a Little Pig.") You should make copies of the poem for each student in your class
3. Choose a favorite kitten story (either a personal pet story of your own or another story you have read to students before). Be prepared to share this story with students
4. If you do not have computers with Internet access in your classroom, reserve a session in your school's computer lab.
5. Visit and familiarize yourself with the Flip Book tool. You may want to arrange for older students who understand this tool to work one-on-one with your class during the Technology session. These can be your students' "technology buddies
6. Read the poem you have chosen to your students at least once prior to the lesson so that they are familiar with it. Allow them time to tell what they like or find interesting about the nursery rhyme. Your goal is for students to be familiar with the text.

Instruction and Activities

Vocabulary and Background (20 minutes)

2. Read the nursery rhyme to students. During this part of the session, students should be encouraged to make connections to their lives, other things they have read, or the world. Questions for discussion include:
   - Do any of you have a kitten or a cat?
1. Show students the chart paper with the nursery rhyme "Kittens" written on it (see Preparation, step What color is its nose?
3. Share the pet story you have chosen (see Preparation, Step 3). Ask students if they have had any similar experiences. Allow them time to discuss their own stories
4. Tell students that there is a word in the nursery rhyme "Kittens" that may be unfamiliar; ask them if they can tell you what word it is. The word is slumber

5. Tell students you think that you can figure out what slumber means together. Have them help you make a list of the kinds of things a kitten does. Write the list on a piece of chart paper. Some responses may include: play with string, chase birds, take naps, or climb trees or furniture.
6. When the list has several characteristics, including some version of sleeping, read through it for the class. Ask them if they have a guess as to which item on the list is a definition of slumber, working until they have selected the correct answer. Praise them for their list and correct response.
7. Ask students why it is important to sleep. Talk about the different kinds of slumber there are (e.g., naps, sleeping all night, hibernation). Use the word in a different context, for example: "The bear woke up from his deep winter slumber.

Print Concepts (20 minutes)

1. Gather students in the designated group meeting area. Tell them that you will be rereading "Kittens." Ask them what they remember about reading it before, and what it was about.
2. Show students the chart paper with the poem written on it (see Preparation, Step 2). Ask a student where you will start reading the nursery rhyme. (Have him or her come up and point to the proper place.) Then read the nursery rhyme aloud while you indicate the words with a pointer.
3. Ask a student to come up and point to the words in the nursery rhyme as the entire class reads it aloud chorally. The student you choose may either be one that understands one-to-one matching or one who does not. If you choose the latter, be sure to offer assistance by pointing with the student.
4. Ask students if they see any words they know. Any letters? Have individual students come up and point to the word or letter with a pointer. Have them tell you what it is. If a student incorrectly identifies a letter or word, praise the attempt and then show the correct letter or word in the poem if it is there. If not, use a white board to write the correct response.
5. Point to the words in the poem as you read through the poem one more time with the entire class.

Rhyme (20 minutes)

1. Ask students to read "Kittens" with you. Have one of the students proficient in one-to-one matching use a pointer to point as the class reads.
2. Ask students what they notice about the words day and play, as you highlight them with highlight tape. Responses might be: they rhyme, they sound alike, they look alike, or they have letters that are the same.
3. Reread the nursery rhyme together. Write day and play on a piece of chart paper. Have the class repeat the words a few times.

4. Ask them to try and think of other words that rhyme with these two, writing correct responses on the list and incorrect responses on a white board.
5. Reread the list several times; after every two new additions is a good estimate. Continue adding to the list until there are a handful of correct responses.
6. At this point in the session, one of the students may have already pointed out that call and all rhyme as well; however, if no one has, ask students if there are any other rhyming words. Read the poem an additional time if necessary.
7. Repeat Steps 4 and 5 with call and all.
8. Application (20 minutes)

CHAPTER III

PHONEMIC AWARENESS

Phonemic awareness, a child's ability to hear, identifies, and manipulates individual sounds (phonemes) in spoken words. contributes to early, emergent reading development. Since phonemic awareness is mastered by most students prior to the third grade, these skills are included only at the K-2 grade level. With regard to phonics, even though there are different approaches to teaching phonics, research findings indicate that comprehensive phonics programs should incorporate explicit and systematic phonics instruction. Phonics programs should provide ample opportunities for children to apply what they are learning about letters and sounds to the reading of words, sentences, and stories. Effective instruction in the early grades includes providing students with a variety of literary genres, including decodable books that contain specific letter-sound words they are learning. Hence, students understand that there is a predictable relationship between sounds and letters in spoken and written language, and in the language found in their favorite books (Reutzel, & Cooper, 2000).

- The expectation for reading at all grade levels is that students will read widely. It is important for all students, including students with disabilities and second language learners, to have multiple opportunities to participate in read-alouds, shared and individual reading of high quality materials. Guided repeated oral reading is an effective way of helping students improves their comprehension and fluency skills. Many studies have found that students who become fluent readers read a great deal (National Reading Panel, 2000). Good readers read and comprehend text using similar strategies. Effective strategies used by successful readers at all grade levels include:
- Drawing from prior knowledge to make meaning from print;
- Creating visual images in one's mind to enhance understanding;
- Monitoring one's own reading and checking for understanding;
- Asking questions to identify key points in text and remembering them;
- Making conscious inferences about important information presented;
- Synthesizing new information with existing understanding about a topic;
- Summarizing and understanding how different parts of text are related; and Evaluating and forming opinions about ideas presented. Along with the vision statement, offer a framework for classroom instruction and curriculum development. Technology can be used as an effective tool for literacy

tasks, and can facilitate reading comprehension and provide individualized instruction in areas like vocabulary development, phonemic awareness, and word processing.

Standards and Strands

There are five language arts literacy standards, each of which has lettered strands and learning expectations for each grade level in grades K-8, as well as a combined cluster for grades 9-12. The standards and strands are outlined below:

3.1 Reading

A. Concepts About Print

B. Phonological Awareness

C. Decoding and Word Recognition

D. Fluency

E. Reading Strategies (before, during, and after reading)

F. Vocabulary and Concept Development

G. Comprehension Skills and Response to Text

H. Inquiry and Research

3.2 Writing

A. Writing as a Process

B. Writing as a Product

C. Mechanics, Spelling, and Handwriting

D. Writing Forms, Audiences, and Purposes

3.3 Speaking

A. Discussion

B. Questioning (Inquiry) and Contributing

C. Word Choice

D. Oral Presentation

3.4 Listening

A. Active Listening

B. Listening Comprehension

3.5 Viewing and Media Literacy

A. Constructing Meaning

B. Visual and Verbal Messages

C. Living with Media

Yvonne L. Simon

The early elementary school experiences are critical to school success. Five-year-olds enter school with a wide range of abilities, motivation to learn, and preschool and home literacy experiences. It is understood that some schools continue to provide half-day kindergartens, while others provide full-day programs for children. Half-day kindergarten programs should make every effort to address the prescribed grade-level expectations outlined in the curriculum... It may be necessary for administrators to review their existing kindergarten schedule, program, staff needs, or classroom materials in order for all students to achieve these standards.

The revised standards for language arts literacy, along with the vision statement of a school offer a framework for classroom instruction and curriculum development in that specific school. While this is a powerful challenge to students, teachers, principals, and parents, it can be met through a united commitment. The singular goal of increasing student achievement through effective instruction in the skills required to live and work in a 21st century global community is the driving force of this challenge and these standards. The primary grades are building blocks that lay the foundation for learning and skill development so that each succeeding grade builds on the foundation achieved by all students in their efforts to become fluent readers, writers, speakers, listeners, and viewers. As language arts skills spiral and become increasingly sophisticated, students progress through the grades with increased confidence and proficiency in oral and written language, comprehension, and critical thinking skills. Language skills are essential to furthering learning, communication, career development, and the human spirit. Therefore, teachers should be aware of the interconnection between letters and sounds in the English language, know about the various stages children pass through as they develop word fluency and spelling skills, and have a repertoire of instructional strategies and materials readily available to teach students letter-sounds and associations. Similarly, instructors must have a clear understanding of several important terms associated with word recognition.

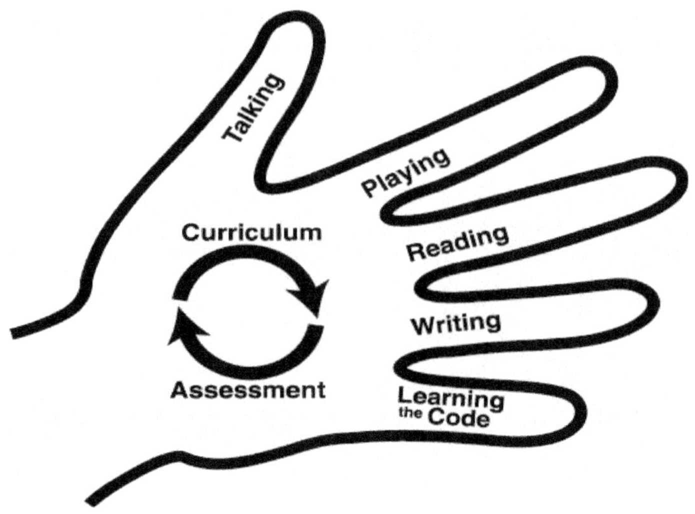

Development Of The Field -Phonology

In ancient India, the Sanskrit grammarian Pāṇini (c. 520–460 BC), who is considered the founder of linguistics, in his text of Sanskrit phonology, the *Shiva Sutras*, discovers the concepts of the phoneme, the morpheme and the root. The *Shiva Sutras* describe a phonemic notational system in the fourteen initial lines of the *Aṣṭādhyāyī*. The notational system introduces different clusters of phonemes that serve special roles in the morphology of Sanskrit, and are referred to throughout the text. Panini's grammar of Sanskrit had a significant influence on Ferdinand de Saussure, the father of modern structuralism, who was a professor of Sanskrit (de Lacy, 2007)

The Polish scholar Jan Baudouin de Courtenay, (together with his former student Mikołaj Kruszewski) coined the word *phoneme* in 1876, and his work, though often unacknowledged, is considered to be the starting point of modern phonology. He worked not only on the theory of the phoneme but also on phonetic alternations (i.e., what is now called allophony and morphophonology). His influence on Ferdinand de Saussure was also significant .Prince Nikolai Trubetzkoy's posthumously published work, the *Principles of Phonology* (1939), is considered the foundation of the Prague School of phonology. Directly influenced by Baudouin de Courtenay, Trubetzkoy is considered the founder of morphophonology, though morphophonology was first recognized by Baudouin de Courtenay. Trubetzkoy split phonology into phonemics and archiphonemics; the former has had more influence than the latter. Another important figure in the Prague School was Roman Jakobson, who was one of the most prominent linguists of the twentieth century (de Lacy, 2007).

In 1968 Noam Chomsky and Morris Halle published *The Sound Pattern of English* (SPE), the basis for Generative Phonology. In this view, phonological representations are sequences of segments made up of distinctive features. These features were an expansion of earlier work by Roman Jakobson, Gunnar Fant, and Morris Halle. The features describe aspects of articulation and perception, are from a universally fixed set, and have the binary values + or -. There are at least two levels of representation: underlying representation and surface phonetic representation. Ordered phonological rules govern how underlying representation is transformed into the actual pronunciation (the so called surface form). An important consequence of the influence SPE had on phonological theory was the downplaying of the syllable and the emphasis on segments. Furthermore, the Generativists folded morphophonology into phonology, which both solved and created problems.

Natural Phonology was a theory based on the publications of its proponent David Stampe (1969) and (more explicitly) in (1979). In this view, phonology is based on a set of universal phonological processes which interact with one another; which ones are active and which are suppressed are language-specific. Rather than acting on segments, phonological processes act on distinctive features within prosodic groups. Prosodic groups can be as small as a part of a syllable or as large as an entire utterance. Phonological processes are unordered with respect to each other and apply simultaneously (though the output of one process may be the input to another). The second-most prominent Natural Phonologist is Stampe's wife, Patricia Donegan; there are many Natural Phonologists in Europe, though also a few others in the U.S., such as Geoffrey Pullum. The principles of Natural Phonology were extended to morphology by Wolfgang U. Dressler, who founded Natural Morphology.

In 1976 John Goldsmith introduced autosegmental phonology. Phonological phenomena are no longer seen as operating on *one* linear sequence of segments, called phonemes or feature combinations, but rather as involving *some parallel sequences* of features which reside on multiple tiers. Autosegmental phonology later evolved into Feature Geometry, which became the standard theory of representation for the theories of the organization of phonology as different as Lexical Phonology and Optimality Theory.

Government Phonology, which originated in the early 1980s as an attempt to unify theoretical notions of syntactic and phonological structures, is based on the notion that all languages necessarily follow a small set of principles and vary according to their selection of certain binary parameters. That is, all languages' phonological structures are essentially the same, but there is restricted variation that accounts for differences in surface realizations. Principles are held to be inviolable, though parameters may sometimes come into conflict. Prominent figures include Jonathan Kaye (Linguist), J. Lowenstamm, et al (1998) formalized in very different ways.

Phonological awareness: a broad category of language, which refers to the awareness of and the ability to manipulate words, syllables, rhymes; and. sounds (Blachman, 2000). Phonological awareness is the knowledge that words are made up of individual sounds. Phonological awareness is the precursor to phonics which is frequently the method used to teach children to read. If a child can not "sound out a word" or does not have good "word attack skills", it is possible that he may not have the underlying phonological awareness skills necessary to understand and use phonics skills. The development of phonological awareness begins during the preschool years. It is not unusual for a child of 4 years to be able to tell a syllable of a word when ask to "tell me a little bit of telephone." Even though she does not know the word syllable, she will say "tel" or "a" or "phone" in response to this request. By 5 years it is not unusual for a child who has been exposed to rhyme to detect a rhyme, that is she will fill in the missing rhyming word in a familiar rhyme. Also by 5 years, most children have memorized poems or finger plays which is also a part of phonological awareness development.

What Are The Phonological Awareness Skills?

1. Syllabification and rhyming as discussed above are the first skills

1. 2. Blending sounds into words such as "f--i---sh" is "fish"

2. 3. Isolating the beginning or ending sounds in a word i.e. "fish" starts with "f" "boat" ends with "t"
3. 4. Segmenting words into sounds i.e. "what sounds are in the word 'dish'-d—i—sh"
4. 5. Deleting the beginning or ending sound and telling what word remains i.e. "say 'beat' now say it again without the 'b'---eat

BY WHAT AGE SHOULD CHILDREN HAVE PHONOLOGICAL AWARENESS SKILLS?

Phonological awareness develops overtime beginning in the preschool years. When children enter kindergarten they are generally expected to be able to syllabicate and rhyme words. Children entering first grade are generally expected to be able to blend sounds into words and to isolate the beginning sound in a word. During first grade the child will learn to isolate the last sound in the word and may begin to segment familiar words into the individual sounds. By the end of second grade a child should be segmenting all sounds into individual sounds and delete beginning or ending sounds and tell the remaining word. The second grade child will also be expected to perform all of these tasks with sound cluster (i.e. 'st', 'ft', 'sk' etc.) d sounds

- Phonemic awareness: the ability to think analytically about the sounds in words. Most phonemic awareness tasks are purely oral.

1. the **ability to hear and manipulate the sounds in spoken words and the understanding that spoken words and syllables are made up of sequences of speech sounds.**
2. **essential to learning to read in an alphabetic writing system, because letters represent sounds or phonemes. Without phonemic awareness, phonics makes little sense.**
3. **fundamental to mapping speech to print. If a child cannot hear that "man" and "moon" begin with the same sound or cannot blend the sounds /rrrrrruuuuuunnnnn/ into the word "run", he or she may have great difficulty connecting sounds with their written symbols or blending sounds to make a word.**
4. essential to learning to read in an alphabetic writing system
5. a strong predictor of children who experience early reading success.

The best predictor of reading difficulty in kindergarten or first grade is the inability to segment words and syllables into constituent sound units (phonemic awareness)

What is a Phoneme?	Different Linguistic Units: Large to Small
Phonemes are the smallest units composing spoken language. (National Reading Panel, 2000) Sun has 3 phonemes: s....u....n	Sentences: The sun shone brightly. Word: sun Syllables: sun, sun-shine, sun-ny Onset-rime: s-un, s-unshine, s-unny Phoneme: s-u-n, s-u-n-sh-i-ne; s-u-nn-y

Why Is Phonemic Awareness Important?

Phonemic Awareness (PA) is important because:

- It requires readers to notice how letters represent sounds. It primes readers for print.
- It gives readers a way to approach sounding out and reading new words.
- It helps readers understand the alphabetic principle (that the letters in words are systematically represented by sounds).

Phonemic Awareness (PA) is difficult because:

- Although there are 26 letters in the English language, there are approximately 40 phonemes, or sound units, in the English language. (NOTE: the number of phonemes varies across sources.)
- Sounds are represented in 250 different spellings (e.g., /f/ as in ph, f, gh, ff).
- The sound units (phonemes) are not inherently obvious and must be taught. The sounds that make up words are "coarticulated;" that is, they are not distinctly separate from each other.

Why Is Phonemic Awareness Important?

Research says:

- The ability to hear and manipulate phonemes plays a causal role in the acquisition of beginning reading skills.
- There is considerable evidence that the primary difference between good and poor readers lies in the good reader's phonological processing ability.
- The effects of training phonological awareness and learning to read are mutually supportive.
- Phonological awareness is teachable and promoted by attention to instructional variables.

Teaching Phonemic Awareness: Critical features of Phonemic Awareness Instruction

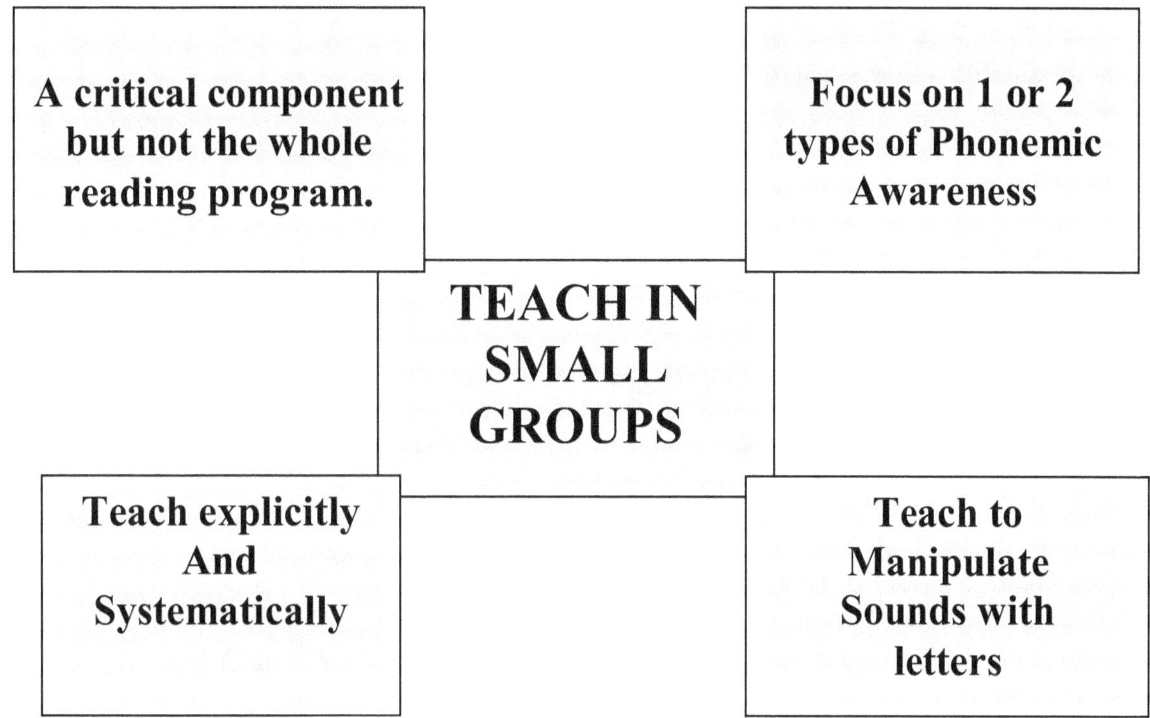

Phonemic Awareness is a critical component of reading instruction but not an entire reading program. It absolutely needs to be taught, but should only be 10-15 minutes per day of your reading instruction.

1. If you focus on just a few types of phonemic awareness, you get better results. There are a lot of skills in phonemic awareness, but research has found that blending and segmentation are the 2 critical skills that must be taught. Instruction must focus on blending and segmenting words at the phoneme, or sound level. This is an auditory task.
2. Research has found that you get better results when teaching phonemic awareness to small groups of children rather than an entire class.
3. Phonemic awareness needs to be taught *explicitly*. The instructional program must show children what they are expected to do. Teachers must model skills they want children to perform before the children are asked to demonstrate the skill.
4. Teachers increase effectiveness when the manipulation of letters is added to phonemic awareness tasks. Phonemic awareness is an *auditory skill,* but once children start to become familiar with the concept, teachers can introduce letter tiles or squares and manipulate them to form sounds and words.

CRITICAL PHONEMIC AWARENESS SKILLS STUDENTS SHOULD LEARN

1. Sound Isolation

   Example: The first sound in *sun* is /ssss/.

2. Blending

   Example: /sss/ - / uuu/ - /nnn/ is *sun.*

3. Segmenting

   Example: The sounds in *sun* are /sss/ - /uuu/ - /n

SEQUENCING PHONEMIC AWARENESS SKILLS

Phonemic awareness instruction typically spans two years, kindergarten and first grade. Oral activities in kindergarten focus on simple tasks such as rhyming, matching words with beginning sounds, and blending sounds into words. In first grade, phonemic awareness tasks are more advanced, focusing on blending ("Blend these sounds together "mmmm-aaaa-nnnn), segmentation ("What are the sounds in man?), and the substitution and manipulation of phonemes (e.g., Change the first sound in man to /r/. What word do you have?").\

PHONOLOGICAL AWARENESS DEVELOPMENT CONTINUUM

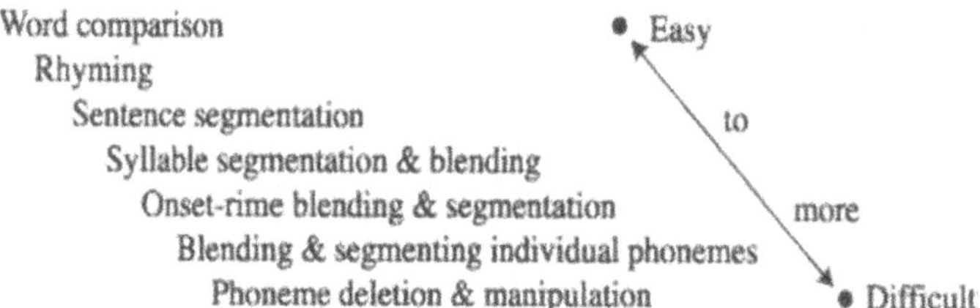

Sequencing Phonemic Awareness skills

Examples of phonemic awareness skills:

- **Sound and Word discrimination**: What word doesn't belong with the others: "cat", "mat", "bat", "ran"? **"ran"**
- **Rhyming**: What word rhymes with "cat"? **bat**
- **Syllable splitting**: The onset of "cat" is /k/, the rime is /at/.
- **Blending**: What word is made up of the sounds /k/ /a/ /t/? **"cat"**
- **Phonemic segmentation**: What are the sounds in "cat"? **/k/ /a/ /t/**
- **Phoneme deletion**: What is "cat" without the /k/? **"at"**
- **Phoneme manipulation**: What word would you have if you changed the /t/ in cat to an /n/? **"can"**

Curriculum Maps:

Phonemic awareness skills can be taught in a particular sequence that maximizes student understanding and instructional efficiency. Phonemic awareness is only taught in kindergarten and first grade. By the end of first grade, students should have a firm grasp of phonemic awareness. Curriculum maps list specific skills that relate to each big idea. Each skill can be taught during at an optimal time during the school year.

How to read curriculum maps

The numbers in the top row of the curriculum map correspond to the months of the school year. For example, if your school year begins in September, then September would be month 1 on the map. If your school year begins in August, then August would be month one. The shaded boxes marked with "X" represent the months in which a particular skill should be taught. The map can be read using either a "horizontal trace" or a "vertical trace". To do a horizontal trace, you select a skill you are interested in, and then trace across the row to find the months marked with an "X" for that skill. This will tell you which months a skill should be taught. To perform a vertical trace, select a particular month, then trace down the column to find the shaded boxes. The shaded boxes correspond to the skills that should be taught that month.

Mapping of Instruction to Achieve Instructional Priorities Kindergarten

Instructional Priority: **Phonemic Awareness**	1	2	3	4	5	6	7	8	9
Focus 1: Sound and Word Discrimination									
1a: Tells whether words and sounds are the same or different	X	X							
1b: Identifies which word is different		X	X						
1c: Identifies which word is different			X	X					
Focus 2: Rhyming b									
2a: Identifies whether words rhyme	X								
2b: Produces a word that rhymes		X	X						
Focus 3: Blending									
3a: Orally blends syllables or onset-rimes			X	X					
3b: Orally blends separate phonemes					X	X	X		
Focus 4: Segmentation									

4a: Clasps words in sentences	X								
4b: Claps syllables in words		X	X						
4c: Says syllables				X	X				
*4d: Identifies first sound in 1-syllable words		X	X	X	25				
4e: Segments individual sounds in words					X	X	X	X	35a

*High priority skill

a. Sounds per minute

b. Optimal time for rhyme Instruction not established

Mapping of Instruction to Achieve Instructional Priorities First Grade

Instructional Priority: **Phonemic Awareness**	1	2	3	4	5	6	7	8	9
Focus 1:: Sound Isolation									
1a: Identifies initial sound in 1-syllable words	X	X							
1b: Identifies : final sound in 1-syllable words	X	X	X						
1c: Identifies medial sound in 1-syllable words		X	X	X					
Focus 2: Sound Blending									
*2a: Blends 3-4 phonemes into a whole word	X	X	X	X	X				
Focus 3: Sound Segmentation									
*3a: Segments 3- and 4-phoneme, 1-syllable words	35 (b)								

* High priority skill

a. Skills in this category should be established by mid-year.

b. Number of phoneme segments per minute

Kindergarten

Students Should Demonstrate These Skills at the End of Kindergarten:

1. **Sound and Word Discrimination**
    - Tells whether words or sounds are the same or different (cat/cat = same; cat/car=different).

- Identifies which word is different (e.g., sun, fun, sun).
- Tells the difference between single speech sounds (e.g., Which one is different? s, s, k).

2. **Rhyming**
   - Identifies whether words rhyme (e.g., cat/mat; ring/sing).
   - Produces a word that rhymes with another (e.g., "A word that rhymes with ***rose*** is ***nose.*** Tell me another word that rhymes with ***rose.)***
3. **Blending**
   - Orally blends syllables (mon-key) or onset-rimes (m-ilk) into a whole word.
   - Orally blends 2-3 separately spoken phonemes into one-syllable words (e.g., m-e: me; u-p: up; f-u-n: fun).
4. **Segmentation**
   - Claps or counts the words in a 3-5 word sentence (e.g., Sue can jump far).
   - Claps or counts the syllables in 1-, 2-, and 3-syllable words.
   - Says each syllable in 2- and 3-syllable words (di-no-saur).
   - Identifies the first sound in a one-syllable word (e.g., /m/ in man).
   - Segments individual sounds in 2- and 3-phoneme, one-syllable words (e.g., run: /r/ /u/ /n/; feet: /f/ /ee/ /t/).

Phonological Awareness Benchmarks for kindergarten:

- 25 first sounds per minute by mid-year
- 35 sound segments per minute by the end of kindergarten.

FIRST GRADE

Students Should Demonstrate These Skills by the Middle of First Grade:

1. **Sound Isolation**
   - Identifies initial sounds in one-syllable words.
   - Identifies final sounds in one-syllable words.
   - Identifies medial sounds in one-syllable words.
2. **Sound Blending**
   - Blends 3-4 phonemes into a whole word (e.g., /m/ /a/ /n/: man; /s/ /k/ /i/ /p/: skip).
3. **Sound Segmentation**
   - Segments 3- and 4-phoneme, one-syllable words (e.g., m-a-n; s-k-i-p).

Phonological Awareness Benchmark for first grade:

35-45 first sounds per minute by mid-year.

Extensions of Segmenting

By the end of grades 1 and 2, students should be able to demonstrate the following skills:

1. Substituting

   Example: "*Nap*. What word do we get when we change the /n/ to /c/?" (as in rhyming or word family practice).

2. Deleting

   Example: "*Flake*. What word do we get when we take away /l/ from *flake?*"

3. Adding

   Example: "*Mile*. What word do we get when we add /s/ to the front of *mile?*"

Assessing Phonemic

Awareness Phonemic awareness should be assessed from the beginning of kindergarten through the spring of first grade.

- **All students** should be assessed a minimum of three times per year to be sure adequate progress toward end of year goals is made.

Students who are identified as at risk of reading difficulty should be monitored 1 or 2 times per month to ensure effectiveness of intervention and to allow timely instructional changes Phonemic Awareness skills can be assessed using standardized measures. The DIBELS assessment system provides two measures that can be used to assess phonemic segmentation skills, Initial Sounds Fluency (ISF) and Phonemic Segmentation Fluency (PSF) Teaching reading comprehension to struggling and at-risk readers today is different from the past. Teachers need to focus on extensive comprehension instruction with all students, not just successful readers.

Struggling readers may come from underprivileged literacy environments, leading to fewer oral language and emergent literacy skills, and limited prior knowledge (Brownell, 2000; and Brooks, 1997). Some parents of the targeted group in the study rarely take time to read to their children, or may not have the ability to do so according to students. This challenges the ability of teachers to successfully educate students (Brooks, 2004). Struggling and at-risk readers may have fewer schemas to help them comprehend while reading. Teachers need to increase schema in the classroom as much as possible. Learning dispositions can be the greatest obstacle to learning, possibly sabotaging the learning possibilities of reading experiences (Kidd Villaume, 2002). Struggling readers differ from skilled readers in their use of world knowledge while comprehending texts, as well as monitoring comprehension and fix-up strategies (Parker, 2002). For some, they lack the knowledge needed in order to rectify their breakdown in comprehension (Massey, 2003). They may fail to understand keywords, and the way that sentences relate to one another (Parker, 2002). Comprehension problems may also be due to difficulties in reading fluently (Parker, 2002). Fluency is vital for students to develop effective reading comprehension skills (Brownell, 2000).

Readers lacking fluency spend excessive time decoding, leading to less short-term memory available for comprehension (Brownell, 2000).Students need to be able to decode well, in order to comprehend the text (Pardo, 2004).Regular independent reading time must be provided for the students to practice the strategies (Pardo, 2004). Dr. Michael Pressley stated the following, "Reading becomes better with practice, and comprehending becomes better with more reading practice" (Pardo, 2004).Other issues that struggling readers need to overcome include: low-quality literature, boring reading materials, and inferior classroom instruction (Brownell, 2000).

Struggling readers require support for many years, however different types of support are needed at different times in a child's reading development (Brownell, 2000). It is imperative that teachers teach decoding skills, build fluency, build prior knowledge, teach new vocabulary, motivate, and engage students with the text in order to improve reading comprehension (Pardo, 2004).

Although one particular strategy may be well suited for one reader, it may not work for another (Brooks, 2004). Therefore, teachers need to assess the strengths of their students, and build on their weaknesses (Wade, 1990). Strategies should be introduced one to two at a time, gradually increasing in number for students that are new to strategy instruction (Brownell, 2000). Teachers teaching the strategies should integrate their strategy instruction into their ongoing teaching (Brownell, 2000).

According to Raphael et. al., there are three principles of reading comprehension instruction.

First, it is imperative that comprehension instruction is explicit. Second, the strategies must be modeled by skillful readers including teachers and peers. Last, the strategies must be scaffolded by teachers until the students are able to use the strategies successfully while independently reading (Raphael, 2004). Efficiency is critical when teaching at-risk students (Carnine et. al., 2006). This can best be achieved by placing student in an instructional group with others that are at their instructional reading level (Carnine et. al., 2006). If possible, at-risk students should receive extra instructional reading time daily, with the amount of time depending on the grade level and how far the child is below grade level (Carnine et. al., 2006).

Although it is definitely important for teachers to explicitly model the strategies, they need to also correct any confusion that emerges while students try out their newly gained strategies (Kidd Villaume, 2002). It is imperative that teachers remind their students about strategy use, if their students neglect to use the strategies on their own, emphasizing that strong readers use strategies (Brownell, 2000). It is of great importance to explain to students that each single strategy makes up only a small part of what skilled readers do while reading (Kidd Villaume, 2002).

Strands and Cumulative Progress Indicators

By the end of Kindergarten, students will:

A. Concepts About Print

1. Realize that speech can be recorded in words (e.g., his/her own name; words and symbols in the environment).
2. Distinguish letters from words.
3. Recognize that words are separated by spaces.
4. Follow words left to right and from top to bottom.
5. Recognize that print represents spoken language.
6. Demonstrate understanding of the function of a book and its parts, including front and back and title page.

B. Phonological Awareness (includes phonemic awareness)

1. Demonstrate understanding that spoken words consist of sequences of phonemes.
2. Demonstrate phonemic awareness by rhyming, clapping syllables, and substituting sounds.
3. Understand that the sequence of letters in a written word represents the sequence of sounds (phonemes) in a spoken word (alphabetic principle).
4. Learn many, though not all, one-to-one letter-sound correspondences.
5. Given a spoken word, produce another word that rhymes with it.

C. Decoding and Word Recognition

1. Recognize some words by sight.
2. Recognize and name most uppercase and lowercase letters of the alphabet.
3. Recognize and read one's name.

D. Fluency

1. Practice reading behaviors such as retelling, reenacting, or dramatizing stories.
2. Recognize when a simple text fails to make sense when listening to a story read aloud.
3. Attempt to follow along in book while listening to a story read aloud.
4. Listen and respond attentively to literary texts (e.g., nursery rhymes) and functional texts (e.g., science books).

E. Reading Strategies (before, during, and after reading)

1. Begin to track or follow print when listening to a familiar text being read.

2. Think ahead and make simple predictions about text.
3. Use picture clues to aid understanding of story content.
4. Relate personal experiences to story characters' experiences, language, customs, and cultures with assistance from teacher.
5. "Read" familiar texts from memory, not necessarily verbatim from the print alone.

F. Vocabulary and Concept Development

1. Continue to develop a vocabulary through meaningful, concrete experiences.
2. Identify and sort words in basic categories.
3. Explain meanings of common signs and symbols.
4. Use new vocabulary and grammatical construction in own speech.

G. Comprehension Skills and Response to Text

1. Respond to a variety of poems and stories through movement, art, music, and drama.
2. Verbally identify the main character, setting, and important events in a story read aloud.
3. Identify favorite books and stories.
4. Retell a story read aloud using main characters and events.
5. Participate in shared reading experiences.
6. Make predictions based on illustrations or portions of stories.

H. Inquiry and Research

1. Locate and know the purposes for various literacy areas of the classroom and the library/media center.
2. Choose books related to topics of interest.

Building upon knowledge and skills gained in the preceding grade, by the end of Grade 1, students will:

A. Concepts About Print

1. Match oral words to printed words (e.g., pointing to print as one reads).
2. Practice reading print in the environment at school and at home with assistance.
3. Locate and identify the title, author, and illustrator of a book or reading selection.
4. Interpret simple graphs, charts, and diagrams.

B. Phonological Awareness (includes phonemic awareness)

1. Demonstrate understanding of all sound- symbol relationships.
2. Blend or segment the phonemes of most one-syllable words.
3. Listen and identify the number of syllables in a word.

4. Merge spoken segments into a word.
5. Add, delete, or change sounds to change words (e.g., cow to how, cat to can).

C. Decoding and Word Recognition

1. Identify all consonant sounds in spoken words (including blends such as bl, br; and digraphs such as th, wh).
2. Recognize and use rhyming words to reinforce decoding skills.
3. Decode regular one-syllable words and nonsense words (e.g., sit, zot).
4. Use sound-letter correspondence knowledge to sound out unknown words when reading text.
5. Recognize high frequency words in and out of context.
6. Decode unknown words using basic phonetic analysis.
7. Decode unknown words using context clues.

D. Fluency

1. Answer questions correctly that are posed about stories read.
2. Begin to read simple text with fluency.
3. Read with fluency both fiction and nonfiction that is grade-level appropriate.

E. Reading Strategies (before, during, and after reading)

1. Use prior knowledge to make sense of text.
2. Establish a purpose for reading and adjust reading rate.
3. Use pictures as cues to check for meaning.
4. Check to see if what is being read makes sense.
5. Monitor their reading by using fix-up strategies (e.g., searching for clues).
6. Use graphic organizers to build on experiences and extend learning.
7. Begin to apply study skills strategies (e.g., survey, question, read, recite, and review—SQ3R) to assist with retention and new learning.

F. Vocabulary and Concept Development

1. Develop a vocabulary of 300-500 high-frequency sight words and phonetically regular words.
2. Use and explain common antonyms and synonyms.
3. Comprehend common and/or specific vocabulary in informational texts and literature.

G. Comprehension Skills and Response to Text

1. Draw simple conclusions from information gathered from pictures, print, and people.
2. Demonstrate familiarity with genres of text, including storybooks, expository texts, poetry, and newspapers.
3. Sequence information learned from text into a logical order to retell facts.
4. Identify, describe, compare, and contrast the elements of plot, setting, and characters.

5. Make simple inferences.
6. Read regularly in independent-level materials.
7. Engage in silent independent reading for specific purposes.

H. Inquiry and Research

1. Ask and explore questions related to a topic of interest.
2. Draw conclusions from information and data gathered.
3. Be exposed to and read a variety of fiction and nonfiction, and produce evidence of reading.

Building upon knowledge and skills gained in preceding grades, by the end of Grade 2, students will:

A. Concepts About Print/Text

1. Use titles, tables of contents, and chapter headings to locate information.
2. Recognize the purpose of a paragraph.

B. Phonological Awareness (includes phonemic awareness)

1. Add, delete, or change middle sounds to change words (e.g., pat to put).
2. Use knowledge of letter-sound correspondences to sound out unknown words.

C. Decoding and Word Recognition

1. Look for known chunks or small words to attempt to decode an unknown word.
2. Reread inserting the beginning sound of the unknown word.
3. Decode regular multisyllable words and parts of words (e.g., capital, Kalamazoo).
4. Read many irregularly spelled words and such spelling patterns as diphthongs, special vowel spellings and common endings.

D. Fluency

1. Pause at appropriate end points (e.g., comma, period).
2. Use appropriate pace; "not choppy" or word-by-word.
3. Use appropriate inflection (e.g., dialogue, exclamations, and questions).
4. Read silently without finger or lip movement.
5. Self-monitor when text does not make sense.
6. Employ learned strategies to determine if text makes sense without being prompted.

E. Reading Strategies (before, during, and after reading)

1. Skip over difficult words in an effort to read on and determine meaning.
2. Return to the beginning of a sentence and try again.

F. Vocabulary and Concept Development

1. Develop a vocabulary of 500-800 regular and irregular sight words.

2. Know and relate meanings of simple prefixes and suffixes.
3. Demonstrate evidence of expanding language repertory.
4. Understand concept of antonyms and synonyms.
5. Begin to use a grade-appropriate dictionary with assistance from teacher.

G. Comprehension Skills and Response to Text

1. Demonstrate ability to recall facts and details of text.
2. Recognize cause and effect in text.
3. Make inferences and support them with textual information.
4 Continue to identify story elements in text.
5. Respond to text by using how, why, and what-if questions.

H. Inquiry and Research

1. Locate information using alphabetical order.
2. Read a variety of nonfiction and fiction books and produce evidence of reading.

Building upon knowledge and skills gained in preceding grades, by the end of Grade 3, students will:

A. Concepts About Print/Text

1. Recognize that printed materials provide specific information.
2. Recognize purposes for print conventions such as end-sentence punctuation, paragraphing, and bold print.
3. Use a glossary or index to locate information in a text.

B. Phonological Awareness (includes phonemic awareness)

1. Demonstrate a sophisticated sense of sound-symbol relationships, including all phonemes (e.g. blends, digraphs, diphthongs).

C. Decoding and Word Recognition

1. Know sounds for a range of prefixes and suffixes (e.g., re-, ex-, -ment, -tion).
2. Use letter-sound knowledge and structural analysis to decode words.
3. Use context to accurately read words with more than one pronunciation.

D. Fluency

1. Recognize grade-level words accurately and with ease so that a text sounds like spoken language when read aloud.

2. Read longer text and chapter books independently and silently.
3. Read aloud with proper phrasing, inflection, and intonation.

E. Reading Strategies (before, during, after reading)

1. Set purpose for reading and check to verify or change predictions during/after reading.
2. Monitor comprehension and accuracy while reading in context and self-correct errors.
3. Use pictures and context clues to assist with decoding of new words.
4. Develop and use graphic organizers to build on experiences and extend learning.

F. Vocabulary and Concept Development

1. Spell previously studied words and spelling patterns accurately.
2. Point to or clearly identify specific words or wording that cause comprehension difficulties.
3. Infer word meanings from taught roots, prefixes, and suffixes.
4. Use a grade-appropriate dictionary with assistance from teacher.
5. Use pictures and context clues to assist with meaning of new words.

G. Comprehension Skills and Response to Text

1. Recognize purpose of the text.
2. Distinguish cause/effect, fact/opinion, and main idea/supporting details in interpreting texts.
3. Interpret information in graphs, charts, and diagrams.
4. Ask how, why, and what-if questions in interpreting nonfiction texts.
5. Recognize how authors use humor, sarcasm, and imagery to extend meaning.
6. Discuss underlying theme or message in interpreting fiction.
7. Summarize major points from fiction and nonfiction texts.
8. Draw conclusions and inferences from texts.
9. Recognize first-person "I" point of view.
10. Compare and contrast story plots, characters, settings, and themes.
11. Participate in creative responses to texts (e.g., dramatizations, oral presentations).
12. Read regularly in materials appropriate for their independent reading level.
13. Read and comprehend both fiction and nonfiction that is appropriately designed for grade level.
14. Use information and reasoning to examine bases of hypotheses and opinions.

H. Inquiry and Research

1. Use library classification systems, print or electronic, to locate information.
2. Draw conclusions from information and data gathered.
3. Read a variety of nonfiction and fiction books and produce evidence of understanding.

Building upon knowledge and skills gained in preceding grades, by the end of Grade 4, students will:

A. Concepts About Print/Text

1. Identify differences of various print formats, including newspapers, magazines, books, and reference resources.
2. Recognize purposes and uses for print conventions such as paragraphs, end-sentence punctuation, and bold print.
3. Identify and locate features that support text meaning (e.g., maps, charts, illustrations).

B. Phonological Awareness

No additional indicators at this grade level.

C. Decoding and Word Recognition

1. Use letter-sound correspondence and structural analysis (e.g., roots, affixes) to decode words.
2. Know and use common word families to decode unfamiliar words.
3. Recognize compound words, contractions, and common abbreviations.

D. Fluency

1. Use appropriate rhythm, flow, meter, and pronunciation in demonstrating understanding of punctuation marks.
2. Read at different speeds using scanning, skimming, or careful reading as appropriate.

E. Reading Strategies (before, during, and after reading)

1. Use knowledge of word meaning, language structure, and sound-symbol relationships to check understanding when reading.
2. Identify specific words or passages causing comprehension difficulties and seek clarification.
3. Select useful visual organizers before, during, and after reading to organize information (e.g., Venn diagrams).

F. Vocabulary and Concept Development

1. Infer word meanings from learned roots, prefixes, and suffixes.
2. Infer specific word meanings in the context of reading passages.
3. Identify and correctly use antonyms, synonyms, homophones, and homographs.
4. Use a grade-appropriate dictionary (independently) to define unknown words.

G. Comprehension Skills and Response to Text

1. Discuss underlying themes across cultures in various texts.
2. Distinguish cause and effect, fact and opinion, main idea, and supporting details in nonfiction texts (e.g., science, social studies).
3. Cite evidence from text to support conclusions.

4. Understand author's opinions and how they address culture, ethnicity, gender, and historical periods.
5. Follow simple multiple-steps in written instructions.
6. Recognize an author's point of view.
7. Identify and summarize central ideas in informational texts.
8. Recognize differences among forms of literature, including poetry, drama, fiction, and nonfiction.
9. Recognize literary elements in stories, including setting, characters, plot, and mood.
10. Identify some literary devices in stories.
11. Identify the structures in poetry.
12. Identify the structures in drama.
13. Read regularly in materials appropriate for their independent reading level.

H. Inquiry and Research

1. Use library classification systems, print or electronic, to locate information.
2. Investigate a favorite author and produce evidence of research.
3. Read independently and research topics using a variety of materials to satisfy personal, academic, and social needs, and produce evidence of reading.

Building upon knowledge and skills gained in preceding grades, by the end of Grade 5, students will:

A. Concepts About Print/Text

1. Use a text index and glossary appropriately.
2. Survey and explain text features that contribute to comprehension (e.g., headings, introductory and concluding paragraphs).

B. Phonological Awareness

No additional indicators at this grade level.

C. Decoding and Word Recognition

1. Use the pronunciation key of a dictionary to decode new words.
2. Use context clues or knowledge of phonics, syllabication, prefixes, and suffixes to decode new words.
3. Interpret new words correctly in context.
4. Apply spelling and syllabication rules that aid in decoding and word recognition.

D. Fluency

1. Adjust reading speed appropriately for different purposes and audiences.

2. Apply knowledge of letter-sound associations, language structures, and context to recognize words.
3. Read aloud in ways that reflect understanding of proper phrasing and intonation.
4. Read silently for the purpose of increasing speed, accuracy, and reading fluency.
5. Apply self-correcting strategies to decode and gain meaning from print both, orally and silently.

E. Reading Strategies (before, during, and after reading)

1. Activate prior knowledge and anticipate what will be read or heard.
2. Vary reading strategies according to their purpose for reading and the nature of the text.
3. Reread to make sense of difficult paragraphs or sections of text.
4. Make revisions to text predictions during and after reading.
5. Apply graphic organizers to illustrate key concepts and relationships in a text.

F. Vocabulary and Concept Development

1. Infer word meanings from learned roots, prefixes, and suffixes.
2. Infer specific word meanings in the context of reading passages.
3. Identify and correctly use antonyms, synonyms, homophones, and homographs.
4. Use a grade-level appropriate dictionary independently to define unknown words.
5. Use a thesaurus to identify alternative word choices and meanings.

G. Comprehension Skills and Response to Text

1. Identify author's purpose, views, and beliefs.
2. Identify genre by their distinctive elements (e.g. tall tale-exaggeration).
3. Use cause and effect and sequence of events to gain meaning.
4. Anticipate and construct meaning from text by making conscious connections to self, an author, and others.
5. Recognize persuasive and propaganda techniques used to influence readers.
6. Recognize historical and cultural biases and different points of view.
7. Understand that theme refers to the central idea or meaning of a selection and recognize themes, whether implied or stated directly.
8. Distinguish between major and minor details.
9. Make inferences using textual information and provide supporting evidence.
10. Recognize common organizational patterns in text that support comprehension (e.g., headings, captions).
11. Identify and analyze text types, formats, and elements in nonfiction.
12. Recognize literary elements in stories, including setting, characters, plot, and mood.

13. Recognize figurative language in text (e.g. simile, metaphor, personification, alliteration).
14. Identify and respond to the elements of sound and structure in poetry.
15. Identify the structures in drama.
16. Read regularly in materials appropriate for their independent reading level.
17. Interpret idiomatic expressions.

H. Inquiry and Research

1. Use library classification systems, print or electronic, to locate information.
2. Develop and revise questions for investigations prior to, during, and after reading.
3. Use multiple sources to locate information relevant to research questions.
4. Read independently and research topics using a variety of materials to satisfy personal, academic, and social needs, and produce evidence of reading.
5. Draw conclusions from information gathered from multiple sources.
6. Interpret and use graphic sources of information such as maps, graphs, timelines, or tables to address research questions.
7. Summarize and organize information by taking notes, outlining ideas, and/or making charts.
8. Produce projects and reports, using visuals, media, and/or technology to show learning and support the learning of an audience.

CHAPTER IV

PHONICS (HISTORY AND CONTROVERSY OF PHONICS)

The National Reading Panel (2007) stated that because of the complexity of the English alphabetic structure, more than a century of debate has occurred over whether English phonics ought to be taught at all. Beginning in the mid-19th century, some American educators, prominently Horace Mann, argued this point precisely. This led to the commonly used "look-say" approach ensconced in the "Dick and Jane" readers popular in the mid-20th century. Beginning in the 1950s, however, phonics resurfaced as a method of teaching reading. Spurred by Rudolf Flesch's polarizing, bombastic criticism of the absence of phonics instruction (particularly in his popular book, *Why Johnny Can't Read*) phonics resurfaced, but owing to Flesch's polemical approach the term "phonics" became associated with political ideology. The popularity of phonics rose, but many educators associated it with "back to basics" pedagogy and eschewed it.

In the 1980s, the "whole language" approach to reading further polarized the debate in the United States. Whole language instruction was predicated on the principle that children could learn to read given (a) proper motivation, (b) access to quality literature, (c) many reading opportunities, (d) focus on meaning, and (e) instruction to help students use meaning clues to determine the pronunciation of unknown words. For some advocates of whole language, phonics was the antithesis of this emphasis on getting at the meaning. Parsing words into small chunks and reassembling them had no connection to the ideas the author wanted to convey. Much of the whole language theory easily dovetailed with phonics, but the whole language emphasis on understanding words through context and focusing only a little on the sounds (usually the alphabet consonants and the short vowels) could not be reconciled with the phonics emphasis on individual sound-symbol correspondences. Thus, a false dichotomy between the whole language approach and phonics emerged in the United States, leading to intense debate and ultimately to a Congressionally-commissioned book and two government-funded panels focused on phonics.

The book *Beginning to Read: Thinking and Learning about Print* (Adams, 1990) argued that phonics was an effective way for students to learn to read. Adams argued strongly that both the phonics and the whole language advocates were right. Phonics was an effective way to teach students the alphabetic code. By learning the alphabetic code early, students could quickly free up mental energy they had used to word analysis and devote this mental effort to meaning, leading to stronger comprehension earlier in elementary education. This result matched the goal of whole language instruction while the means supported the advocates of phonics.

The argument, eventually known as "the Great Debate" continued unabated. The National Research Council re-examined the question of phonics (among other questions in education) and published the results of its Committee on the Prevention of Reading Difficulties in Young Children (Snow, Burns, and Griffin, 1998). The National Research Council's findings matched those of Adams. Phonics was a very effective way to teach children to read, more effective than what was known as the "embedded phonics" approach of whole language (where phonics was taught opportunistically in the context of literature). They found that phonics must be systematic (following a sequence of increasingly challenging phonics patterns) and explicit (teaching students precisely how the patterns worked, e.g., "this is *b*; it stands for the /b/ sound").

The most recent attempt to determine what approach made the most sense was undertaken by the National Reading Panel (National Institute of Child Health and Human Development, 2001), which examined quantitative research studies on phonics (as well as other areas of reading instruction). Their meta-analysis of hundreds of studies confirmed the findings of the National Research Council: phonics is a more effective way to teach children to read than is embedded phonics or no phonics instruction. They found that phonics had particularly strong benefits for students of low socio –economic statue.

What Exactly Is Phonics?

Phonics is knowing that sounds and letters have a relationship, it's that simple, and that complex. It is the link between what we say and what we can read and write. Children need very explicit instructions on how the letters on a page correspond to the spoken word. A child who has mastered phonics can connect the sounds he knows with letters, and then put them together to make words. (And then he can put words together to read sentences, and so on.)

Phonics offers your beginning reader the strategies she needs to sound out words. For example, she learns that the letter D has the sound of "d" as in "doll." Then she learns how to blend letter sounds together to make words like *dog*. It's not as easy as it sounds, because the 26 letters in our alphabet correspond to 44 sounds. But when your child has mastered it, this knowledge helps her read familiar words at an appropriate pace, and gives her the ability to decode and spell words she hasn't seen before.

Why Is Phonics Important?

The ultimate goal of reading is good comprehension. On the contrary, in order for your child to understand what he reads, he must be able to do it quickly and automatically, without stumbling over words.

Phonics facilitates that process. With lots of practice sounding out words, in combination with other important reading skills such as phonemic awareness, letter recognition, vocabulary building, and concepts of print, he learns to read more fluently. Then he can turn his attention to grasping the passages.

How Is Phonics Taught?

Phonics is taught systematically and sequentially. Teachers give children plenty of practice before moving on. Your child will read short, easy books, containing the particular letter sounds or words she's working on. "Children need frequent opportunities to read aloud, with the teacher guiding and correcting them," (Abbott, 2000) In addition, there should be lots of writing, to reinforce the sound-print connection. Here's what your child is likely to learn in each grade:

Kindergarten:

- Letter recognition: learning the letters of the alphabet.
- Connecting some letters with their sounds (she'll know about 20 sound-symbol connections by the end of the year).
- Phonemic awareness: understanding that words are made of individual, separate sounds. She may be asked to clap out her name, make up nonsense words, or listen for the rhymes in a poem to build sound sensitivity.
- Reading and writing easy consonant-vowel-consonant words (in some schools).
- A few sight words.

First grade:

- Mastery of short and long vowels
- Letter combinations: The "b" sound plus the "r" sound makes the "br" blend, in which you can still hear both of the consonants you started with; "t" plus "h" makes a new "th" sound
- Reading simple words, sentences and stories
- Beyond phonics: word endings, like "-ed" and "-ing," and more sight words, such as *is, was, have*, and *are*

Second grade:

- Vowel combinations (what sound does "ea" make? How about "ai"?).
- Spelling patterns of increasing difficulty.
- Multisyllabic words and putting word parts together ("pan" plus "cake" equals *pancake*).
- Vocabulary and word recognition

How can I support phonics learning at home?

Reinforce schoolwork with easy activities.

- Team up with the teacher. Ask how you can highlight phonics and reading. If you have concerns, share them. Struggling readers should be given extra-intensive instruction, either in the classroom, or in small groups with the school reading specialist. "Don't be satisfied if the teacher says 'Let's just give it some time,'" emphasizes Dr. Gillis. Children need help as early as possible in order to catch up.
- Listen to your child read daily. "If he stumbles on a word, encourage him to sound it out," nevertheless, if he still can't get it, provide the word so he doesn't get discouraged. Take turns reading a paragraph at a time, to help make it more fun.
- Boost comprehension. Ask questions like, "What do you think will happen next?" or "What did he mean by that?"
- Revisit familiar books. It's okay if your child wants to read favorites from earlier years. "Reading easy books helps kids develop fluency, and assures success in those early stages," If a book has more than five unknown words on a page, it's too challenging, McGowan adds.
- Read aloud. Choose books on topics that excite your child, and read with gusto, using different voices for the characters. This is where you can expose your child to more challenging literature to enrich vocabulary. In the early grades, her listening level far exceeds her reading level.
- Spread the joy. Show your child how much you value reading by having plenty of books and magazines around the house. Furthermore, visit the library and bookstores often. You'll cultivate a lifelong love of reading in your child

Different Phonics Approaches

Synthetic phonics is a method employed to teach phonics to children when learning to read. This method involves examining every spelling within the word individually as an individual sound and then blending those sounds together. For example, *shrouds* would be read by pronouncing the sounds for each spelling "/ʃ, ɹ, aʊ, d, z/" and then blending those sounds orally to produce a spoken word, "/ʃɹaʊdz/." The goal of synthetic phonics instruction is that students identify the sound-symbol correspondences and blend their phonemes automatically. (synthetic phonics)

Analytic phonics has children analyze sound-symbol correspondences, such as the *ou* spelling of /aʊ/ in *shrouds* but students do not blend those elements as they do in synthetic phonics lessons. Furthermore, consonant blends (separate, adjacent consonant phonemes) are taught as units (e.g., in *shrouds* the *shr* would be taught as a unit).

Analogy phonics is a particular type of analytic phonics in which the teacher has students analyzes phonic elements according to the phonograms in the word. A phonogram, known in linguistics as a rime, is composed of the vowel and all the sounds that follow it. Teachers using the analogy method assist students in memorizing a bank of phonograms, such as *-at* or *-am*. Students then use these phonograms to analogize to unknown words.

Embedded phonics is the hallmark of traditional whole language phonics programs. Phonics is taught in the context of literature using "mini-lessons," short lessons that emphasize phonic elements with which the teacher has seen students struggle. The focus on meaning is generally maintained, but the mini-lesson provides some time for focus on individual sounds or phonograms. Embedded phonics differs from other methods in that the instruction is always in the context of literature and that separate lessons are not typically taught.

Owing to the shifting debate over time (see "History and Controversy" above), many school systems, such as California's, have made major changes in the method they have used to teach early reading. Today, most teachers combine phonics with the elements of whole language that focus on reading comprehension, as Adams advocated. This combined approach is often called balanced literacy. Proponents of various approaches generally agree that a combined approach is important. A few stalwarts favor isolated synthetic phonics and introduction of intensive reading comprehension only after children have mastered sound-symbol correspondences. On the other side, some whole language supporters are intransigent in arguing that phonics should be taught little, if at all. Generally, however, the balanced literacy approach has settled much of the disagreement in the United States.

There has been a resurgence in interest in synthetic phonics in recent years, particularly in the United Kingdom. The subject has been promoted by a cross-party group of Parliamentarians, particularly Nick Gibb MP. A recent report by the House of Commons Education and Skills Committee called for a review of the phonics content in the National Curriculum. The Department for Education and Skills has since announced a review into early years reading, headed by Jim Rose. Jim Rose's group has now reported and the UK Government has decreed that synthetic phonics should be the method of choice for teaching reading in primary schools in England. Free phonics programs using synthetic phonics can be found at Don Potter's Education Page and The Phonics Page .Phonics is the core of beginning reading programs like Hooked on Phonics

- Phonics: the systematical relationship between sounds and written symbols. Phonics deals with learning sound-spelling relationships and is associated with print.
- Structural analysis: the large structural units that make up words, prefixes, suffixes, compound words, contractions, and syllables.
- Sight words: words that are recognized quickly, accurately, and effortlessly by the reader.

Teachers should know the meaning of these word recognition terms as well as have a working knowledge of optimal instructional methods and materials needed to teach students to be efficient users of the alphabetic principle. Based on a learner's literacy needs and the text being read, a variety of decoding strategies (sight words, phonics, contextual analysis, structural analysis) should be taught and employed. When approaching a new word in a text, the learner should be questioning: "Should I reread and think about what would make sense?" Does it look right and sound right?" "Why did I stop?" No one technique is effective for decoding every unknown word. Abbott, (2000) states that when a child can decide on his, or her own philosophy, then the most efficient and effective approach, is the various decoding skills that become decoding strategies

ALPHABETIC PRINCIPLE

English spelling is based upon the alphabetic principle, the idea that letters represent sounds. For example, the word *pat* is composed of three letters, *p*, *a*, and *t*, each representing a phoneme, respectively, /p/, /æ/, and /t/.[1] Some letters in English regularly represent one sound, such as *b*, *m*, and *d*. However, the alphabetic principle is not sufficient to represent all of the spellings in English.

Reading in English also requires understanding of additional patterns that do not follow the "one letter–one sound" principle. For example, the word *shirt* is composed of five letters which represent only three sounds, /ʃ/, /ɝ/, and /t/. The connections between spellings (also called graphemes) and sounds are called "sound-symbol correspondences" or "sound-spelling correspondences," among other names.

Sound-symbol correspondences often follow certain conventions, and these conventions are often called "phonics rules" or "phonics patterns." When English spelling rules take into account syllable structure, phonetics, and accents, there are literally dozens of rules that are 75% or more reliable. Additionally, identifying reliable generalizations for spelling words are the importance of multilevel analysis. The Elementary School Journal 101(2), 233-245.

English has many phonics patterns. These vary considerably in the degree to which they follow the stated pattern. For example, the letters *ee* almost always represent /i/. On the other hand, the grapheme *ough* represents /ʌf/ as in *enough*, /oʊ/ as in *though*, /u/ as in *through*, /ɔf/ as in *cough*, and /æɔ/ as in *bough*. Therefore, teachers generally teach that *ee* says /i/ but rarely teach a pattern for the letters *ough*. Because a large body of patterns that constantly conflict is antithetical to students remembering the patterns they are taught, elementary school children often learn a selection of these patterns known to be most consistent. A selection of these is given below, although not all of these are taught by teachers.

Vowel phonics patterns

- Short vowels are the five single letter vowels, a, e, i, o, and u when they produce the sounds /æ/ as in *cat*, /ɛ/ as in *bet*, /ɪ/ as in *sit*, /ɑ/ as in *hot*, and /ʌ/ as in *cup*. The term "short vowel" does not really mean that these vowels are pronounced for a particularly short period of time. The use of the term is more conventional than meaningful.
- Long vowels are synonymous with the names of the single letter vowels, such as /eɪ/ in *baby*, /i/ in *meter*, /ɑɪ/ in *tiny*, /oʊ/ in *broken*, and /ju/ in *humor*. The way that educators use the term "long vowels" differs from the way in which linguists use this term. In classrooms, long vowels sounds are taught as being "the same as the names of the letters."
- Schwa is the third sound that most of the single vowel spellings can produce. The schwa is an indistinct sound of a vowel in an unstressed syllable, represented by the linguistic symbol **ə**. /ə/ is the sound made by the *o* in *lesson*. Schwa is a vowel pattern that is not always taught to elementary school students because it is difficult to understand. However, some educators make the argument that schwa should be included in primary reading programs because of its importance in reading English words (Abbott, 2000)
- Closed syllables are syllables in which a single vowel letter is followed by a consonant. In the word *button*, both syllables are closed syllables because they contain single vowels followed by consonants. Therefore, the letter *u'* represents the short sound /ʌ/. (The *o* in the second syllable makes the /ə/ sound because it is an unstressed syllable.)
- Open syllables are syllables in which a vowel appears at the end of the syllable. The vowel will say its long sound. In the word *basin*, *ba* is an open syllable and therefore says /beɪ/.
- Diphthongs are linguistic elements that fuse two adjacent vowel sounds. English has four common diphthongs. The commonly recognized diphthongs are /aʊ/ as in *cow* and /ɔɪ/ as in *boil*. Four of the long vowels are also technically diphthongs, /eɪ/, /ɑɪ/, /oʊ/, and /ju/, which partly accounts for the reason they are considered "long."
- Vowel digraphs are those spelling patterns wherein two letters are used to represent the vowel sound. The *ai* in *sail* is a vowel digraph. Because the first letter in a vowel digraph sometimes says its long vowel sound, as in *sail*, some phonics programs once taught that "when two vowels go walking, the first one does the talking." This convention has been almost universally discarded, owing to the many non-examples. The *au* spelling of the /ɔ/ sound and the *oo* spelling of the /u/ and /ʊ/ sounds do not follow this pattern.

- Vowel-consonant-E spellings are those wherein a single vowel letter, followed by a consonant and the letter *e* makes the long vowel sound. Examples of this include *bake*, *theme*, *hike*, *cone*, and *cute*. (The *ee* spelling, as in *meet* is sometimes considered part of this pattern.)

Consonant phonics patterns

- Consonant digraphs are those spellings wherein two letters are used to represent a consonant phoneme. The most common consonant digraphs are *ch* for /tʃ/, *ng* for /ŋ/, *ph* for /f/, *sh* for /ʃ/, *th* for /θ/ and /ð/, and *wh* for /ʍ/ (often pronounced /w/ in American English). Letter combinations like *wr* for /ɹ/ and *kn* for /n/ are also consonant digraphs, although these are sometimes considered patterns with "silent letters."
- Short vowel + consonant patterns involve the spelling of the sounds /k/ as in *peek*, /dʒ/ as in *stage*, and /tʃ/ as in *speech*. These sounds each have two possible spellings at the end of a word, *ck* and *k* for /k/, *dge* and *ge* for /dʒ/, and *tch* and *ch* for /tʃ/. The spelling is determined by the type of vowel that precedes the sound. If a short vowel precedes the sound, the former spelling is used, as in *pick*, *judge*, and *match*. If a short vowel does not precede the sound, the latter spelling is used, as in *took*, *barge*, and *launch*.

The final "short vowel + consonant pattern" is just one example of dozens that can be used to help children unpack the challenging English alphabetic code. This example illustrates that, while complex, English spelling retains order and reason.

Sight words and high frequency words

- There is a body of words that do not follow these rules; they are called "sight words". Sight words must be memorized since the regular rules do not apply, *e.g., were*, *who*, *you*.
- Teachers who use phonics also often teach students to memorize the most high frequency words in English, such as *it*, *he*, *them*, and *when*, even though these words are fully decodable. The argument for teaching these "high frequency words" is that knowing them will improve students' reading fluency.

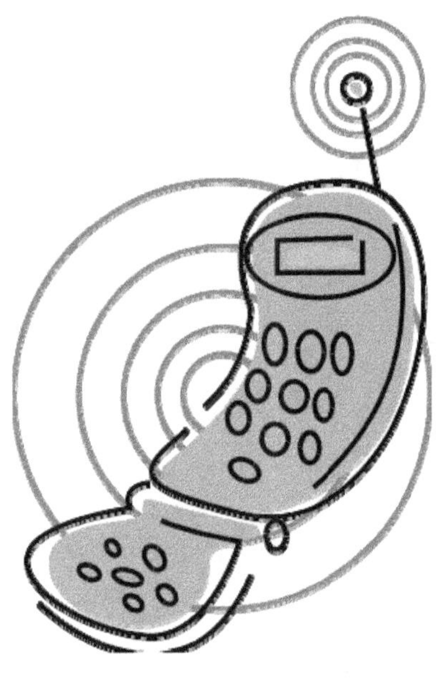

HELLO! MY NAME IS POLLY. CAN YOU teach ME TO READ? I REALLY WANT TO LEARN TO READ. I WOULD LIKE TO BE A PILOT SOMEDAY AND WORK WITH THE UNITED STATES ARMY. PLEASE TEACH ME TO READ.

PHONICS WORKOUT!

Aa - Apple

CHAPTER V

FLUENCY

WHAT IS FLUENCY?

Reading fluency is the ability to read text with speed, accuracy, quickly, and proper expression. Fluency bridges word decoding and comprehension. Comprehension is to understand what has been read. Fluency is a set of skills that allows readers to rapidly decode text while maintaining high comprehension (National Reading Panel, 2001).A first benchmark for fluency is being able to "sight read" some words. The idea is that children will recognize at sight the most common words in written English and that instant reading of these words will allow them to read and understand text more quickly. Also, since there are many common English words that are so irregular according to the rules of phonics, it is best to get children to just memorize them from the start. For example, try sounding out these words: "one", "was", "if", "even", or "the". As children learn to read, the speed at which they read becomes an important measure.

Fluent readers:

- Recognize words automatically
- Read aloud effortlessly and with expression
- Do not have to concentrate on decoding
- Can focus on comprehension

"Fluency is important because it provides a bridge between word recognition and comprehension." (Reading Links, 2002, p. 9). Fluency doesn't ensure comprehension, but comprehension is difficult without fluency. If a reader is constantly stopping to decode and figure out unknown words, most likely meaning will be disrupted and the process of reading becomes long and laborious. When students make gains in reading fluency, they are able to put their energies into comprehension and are able to analyze, interpret, draw conclusions, and infer meaning from texts.

The three components of fluency

- **Accuracy:** Also known as automaticity, it refers to the person's ability to read words in a text.
- **Rate:** The speed a person reads.
- **Prosody:** Refers to stress, intonation, and pauses. Commonly known as "reading with feeling".

In order to implement fluency teaching into reading instruction, teachers need to be aware of the three components of fluency.

Fluency Instruction

Teachers need to select and facilitate the best methods of fluency instruction for their children and their classrooms. The following four components are needed for good fluency instruction.

1. Model fluent reading.
2. Use guided oral reading instruction.
3. Give students ways to practice and perform.
4. Implement word study activities to build accuracy.

Here are some examples of activities for each of the components.

1. Model fluent reading: Students need to hear and see what fluent reading looks like.

- Read Aloud - An adult reads aloud a text to the whole class.
- Books on Tape - Children can listen to stories on tape as they follow along in a book.
- Buddy Reading - An upper grade child reads aloud to a lower grade child.

2. Use guided oral reading instruction: Students need assisted, guided oral reading instruction with a teacher, adult, or a peer.

- Choral Reading - All the students, lead by the teacher, read aloud together.
- Peer/Paired Reading- Students are required to work as pairs. Each student reads their text silently. Then the students take turns reading the passage three times orally to the other student. The listening student acts as the teacher by giving suggestions and feedback.
- Echo Reading - echo reading, the teacher reads a sentence, paragraph, or page aloud and then has the students chorally reread that segment.
- Tape Assisted Reading - Children listen and read along with a tape.
- Buddy Reading - An upper grade student listens to a lower grade student read, giving appropriate feedback.

3. Practice and Performance - Children need lots of practice to learn to read fluently. Performing helps students learn prosody.

- Repeated Reading - Students choose their own appropriate text or the teacher assigns a passage. The teacher discusses reading behaviors such as phrasing, rate, intonation, etc. The students practice their texts several times until fluency has developed. Poems and rhymes are great for repeated reading. There are three ways to provide repeated reading experiences: direct instruction (whole class), independent choice, or assisted method (books on tape).
- Independent Reading - Children choose text on their independent level to read silently.
- Reader's Theater - Reader's Theater is an oral performance of a script usually based on authentic literature. Meaning is conveyed through expression and intonation—students need to interpret the script instead of memorizing it, thus helping with comprehension as well as fluency. Repeated readings, or rehearsals, helps students build fluency in a natural and authentic manner.
- Radio Reading - A form of Reader's Theater, students, with copies of the text, perform in front of class.
- Oral Recitation Lesson - This is a combination of a Reader's Theater and Round Robin Reading. In this strategy, the teacher introduces a new selection with the focus being on comprehension. The teacher reads aloud the text and fosters discussion on the content. After modeling a fluent reading of the text and teaching the comprehension lesson, the teacher selects students to act out the text while the rest of the class reads it from individual copies.

Nursery rhymes, poems, songs, speeches, etc. are great for performing!

4. Word Study - Children need to build their sight word knowledge in order to recognize words quickly when reading.

Using a list of sight words, such as a Fry's 300 Instant Words and or Fry's Instant Phrases and Short Sentences.

- Speed drills
- Flashcard practice
- Word Walls
- Sight Word Bingo
- Vocabulary Activities

Not all students need fluency instruction!

Fluency instruction usually begins in the middle of first grade!

When to Implement Fluency Activities

Here are some ideas on implementing fluency instruction into your curriculum:

- Whole group instruction
- Reading groups

- Literacy Centers
- At Home
- Read Alouds
- Silent Reading Time

Literacy Center Ideas:

- Listening Center - children can listen to books on tape.
- Poetry Center - children copy and read poems.
- Song Center - children learn to read and sing songs.
- Recording Center - children read a story on tape.

ASSESSING FLUENCY

Repeated Reading Rate: A child reads a text. Teacher counts how many words were read correctly in one minute. Child does a few repeated readings of the same text as the teacher charts the progress of child on a graph. These tests for rate.

Miscue Analysis/Running Record: A child is given a passage to read. Teacher has copy of the same passage. Teacher marks incorrect reading or omission of words. These tests for accuracy.

Using either the Repeated Reading or Miscue Analysis, teachers rate students' overall fluency using an Oral Reading Rubric. Many schools are now using DIBELS

Fluency is one of those seemingly simple concepts that reward you well for digging deeper. At the basic level, reading fluency refers to the ability to read text accurately, quickly, and with good expression so that time can be allocated to understanding what is read (Meyer & Felton, 1999). There has been a flurry of attention to reading fluency in the last few years because of a growing realization of its importance in reading comprehension. Simultaneously, many researchers and teachers have become increasingly aware of the number of children who have problems in fluency and comprehension, some of whom have adequate but slow decoding skills.

A brief look at a history of research on reading fluency reveals how complicated and how important it is for reading's development in the child. One of the first researchers who contributed to our understanding of fluency was Cattell (1886), a 19th century psychologist who became intrigued by the discovery that we can read a word (like *tiger*) faster than we name a picture of this pouncing feline creature! Cattell was the first to emphasize that humans become almost "automatic" when they read, much more so than speaking. Learning to read so that it is virtually automatic is an extraordinary achievement by our brain. It represents a unique capacity that humans have to learn something so well that they can do it almost without thinking.

Reading Comprehension: The Components of Reading

In its beginnings, reading fluency is the product of the initial development of accuracy and the subsequent development of automaticity in underlying sub lexical processes, lexical processes, and their integration in single-word reading and connected text. These include perceptual, phonological, orthographic, and morphological processes at the letter-, letter-pattern, and word-level; as well as semantic and syntactic processes at the word-level and connected-text level. After it is fully developed, reading fluency refers to a level of accuracy and rate, where decoding is relatively effortless; where oral reading is smooth and accurate with correct prosody; and where attention can be allocated to comprehension. (Wolf & Katzir-Cohen, 2001, p. 219)

Such a developmental, more encompassing view of reading fluency has, we believe, profound implications for prevention, intervention, and assessment. For, within a developmental perspective, efforts to address fluency must start at the beginning of the reading acquisition process, not after reading is already acquired. Most current fluency instruction tends to work on the connected text levels after reading is acquired. Our current research is aimed at designing and testing a comprehensive, developmentally based fluency intervention that addresses the underlying linguistic systems (e.g., phonology, orthography, semantics) at three levels---letter pattern, word, and connected text (Wolf, Miller, & Donnelly, 2000). Preliminary results show that even children with difficult reading fluency and naming speed deficits make significant gains in fluency and comprehension with such an approach.

When fluent readers read silently, they recognize words automatically. They group words quickly to help them gain meaning from what they read. Fluent readers read aloud effortlessly and with expression. Their reading sounds natural, as if they are speaking. Readers who have not yet developed fluency read slowly, word by word. Their oral reading is choppy and plodding.

Fluency is important because it provides a bridge between word recognition and comprehension. Since fluent readers do not have to concentrate on decoding the words, they can focus their attention on what the text means. They can make connections among the ideas in the text and between the text and their background knowledge. In other words, fluent readers recognize words and comprehend at the same time. Less fluent readers, however, must focus their attention on figuring out the words, leaving them little attention for understanding the text. More fluent focus their attention on making connections among the ideas in a text and between these ideas and their background knowledge. Therefore, they are able to focus on comprehension. Less fluent readers must focus their attention primarily on decoding individual words. Therefore, they have little attention left for comprehending the text.

Fluency develops gradually over considerable time and through substantial practice. At the earliest stage of reading development, students' oral reading is slow and labored because students are just learning to "break the code"--to attach sounds to letters and to blend letter sounds into recognizable words. Even when students recognize many words automatically, their oral reading still may be expressionless, not fluent. To read with expression, readers must be able to divide the text into meaningful chunks. These chunks include phrases and clauses. Readers must know to pause appropriately within and at the ends of sentences and when to change emphasis and tone. For example, a reader who lacks fluency may read, probably in a monotone, a line from Bill Martin Jr.'s ***Bumble Bee, Bumble Bee*** as if it were a list of words rather than a connected text, pausing at inappropriate places:

Bumble/

bee bumble/ see what/

do/

you see.

A fluent reader will read the same line as:

Bumble Bee/

Bumble Bee/

What do you see? /

Fluency is not a stage of development at which readers can read all words quickly and easily. Fluency changes, depending on what readers are reading, their familiarity with the words, and the amount of their practice with reading text. Even very skilled readers may read in a slow, labored manner when reading texts with many unfamiliar words or topics. For example, readers who are usually fluent may not be able to read technical material fluently, such as a textbook about nuclear physics or an article in a medical journal.

A recent large-scale study by the National Assessment of Educational Progress (NAEP) found that 44% of a representative sample of the nation's fourth graders was low in fluency. The study also found a close relationship between fluency and reading comprehension. Students who scored lower on measures of fluency also scored lower on measures of comprehension, suggesting that fluency is a neglected reading skill in many American classrooms, affecting many students' reading comprehension.

Although some readers may recognize words automatically in isolation or on a list, they may not read the same words fluently when the words appear in sentences in connected text. Instant or automatic word recognition is a necessary, but not sufficient, reading skill. Students who can read words in isolation quickly may not be able to automatically transfer this "speed and accuracy." It is important to provide students with instruction and practice in fluency as they read connected text.

What Does Scientifically-Based Research Tell Us About Fluency Instruction?

Researchers have investigated two major instructional approaches related to fluency. In the first approach, repeated and monitored oral reading (commonly called "repeated reading"); students read passages aloud several times and receive guidance and feedback from the teacher. In the second approach, independent silent reading, students are encouraged to read extensively on their own. Key findings from the scientific research on fluency instruction include the following conclusions about these two approaches that are of particular interest and value to classroom teachers.

Repeated and monitored oral reading improves reading fluency and overall reading achievement. Students who read and reread passages orally as they receive guidance and/or feedback become better readers. Repeated oral reading substantially improves word recognition, speed, and accuracy as well as fluency. To a lesser but still considerable extent, repeated oral reading also improves reading comprehension. Repeated oral reading improves the reading ability of all students throughout the elementary school years. It also helps struggling readers at higher grade levels.

Traditionally, many teachers have relied primarily on round-robin reading to develop oral fluency. In round-robin reading, students take turns reading parts of a text aloud (though usually not repeatedly). But round-robin reading in itself does not increase fluency. This may be because students only read small amounts of text, and they usually read this small portion only once. Researchers have found several effective techniques related to repeated oral reading:

- students read and reread a text a certain number of times or until a certain level of fluency is reached. Four rereading are sufficient for most students; and
- oral reading practice is increased through the use of audiotapes, tutors, peer guidance, or other means.

In addition, some effective repeated oral reading techniques have carefully designed feedback to guide the reader's performance.

The Difference Between Fluency And Automaticity

Although the terms automaticity and fluency often are used interchangeably, they are not the same thing.

Automaticity is the fast, effortless word recognition that comes with a great deal of reading practice. In the early stages of learning to read, readers may be accurate but slow and inefficient at recognizing words. Continued reading practice helps word recognition become more automatic, rapid, and effortless. Automaticity refers only to accurate, speedy word recognition, not to reading with expression. Therefore, automaticity (or automatic word recognition) is necessary, but not sufficient, for fluency.

One of the major differences between good and poor readers is the amount of time they spend reading. Many studies have found a strong relationship between reading ability and how much a student reads. On the basis of this evidence, teachers have long been encouraged to promote voluntary reading in the classroom. Teacher-education and reading-education literature often recommends in-class procedures for encouraging students to read on their own, such as Silent Sustained Reading (SSR) or Drop Everything and Read (DEAR).

Research, however, has not yet confirmed whether independent silent reading with minimal guidance or feedback improves reading achievement and fluency. Neither has it proven that more silent reading in the classroom cannot work; its effectiveness without guidance or feedback is as yet unproven. The research suggests that there are more beneficial ways to spend reading instructional time than to have students read independently in the classroom without reading instruction.

Fluency Instruction

How can I help my students become more fluent readers? You can help your students become more fluent readers (1) by providing them with models of fluent reading and (2) by having students repeatedly read passages as you offer guidance. In addition, you can help students improve their fluency by combining reading instruction with opportunities for them to read books that are at their independent level of reading ability.

Model Fluent Reading, And Then Have Students Reread The Text On Their Own.

By listening to good models of fluent reading, students learn how a reader's voice can help written text make sense. Read aloud daily to your students. By reading effortlessly and with expression, you are modeling for your students how a fluent reader sounds during reading.

After you model how to read the text, you must have the students reread it. By doing this, the students are engaging in repeated reading. Usually, having students read a text four times is sufficient to improve fluency. Remember, however, that instructional time is limited, and it is the actual time that students are actively engaged in reading that produces reading gains.

Have other adults read aloud to students. Encourage parents or other family members to read aloud to their children at home. The more models of fluent reading the children hear the better. Of course, hearing a model of fluent reading is not the only benefit of reading aloud to children. Reading to children also increases their knowledge of the world, their vocabulary, their familiarity with written language ("book language"), and their interest in reading.

Have Students Repeatedly Read Passages Aloud With Guidance.

The best strategy for developing reading fluency is to provide your students with many opportunities to read the same passage orally several times. To do this, you should first know what to have your students read. Second, you should know how to have your students read aloud repeatedly.

Modeling Fluent Reading

In the primary grades, you might read aloud from a big book. A big book is an enlarged version of a commercially published book--big enough so that all students can clearly see the text. By pointing to each word as you are reading (using either a pointer or your finger), you can show students where and how you are pausing and how the text shows you when to raise or lower your voice. Occasionally, you can also explain to your students why you are reading in a certain way:

Teacher: Did you hear how I grouped the words "Brown bear/ brown bear"?
That's because the words brown and bear belong together.
And then I paused a little before repeating the words.
Teacher: Did you hear how my voice got louder and more excited right here? That's because the author put in this exclamation mark (point to it) to show that the speaker was excited or enthusiastic about what she was saying.
Then, have the students practice reading the same text.

Independent level text

Relatively easy text for the reader, with no more than approximately 1 in 20 words difficult for the reader (95% success)

Instructional Level Text

Challenging but manageable text for the reader, with no more than approximately 1 in 10 words difficult for the reader (90% success)

Frustration Level Text

Difficult text for the reader, with more than 1 in 10 words difficult for the reader (less than 90% success)

What students should read. Fluency develops as a result of many opportunities to practice reading with a high degree of success. Therefore, your students should practice orally rereading text that is reasonably easy for them, that is, text containing mostly words that they know or can decode easily. In other words, the texts should be at the students' independent reading level. A text is at students' independent reading level if they can read it with about 95% accuracy, or misread only about 1 of every 20 words. If the text is more difficult, students will focus so much on word recognition that they will not have an opportunity to develop fluency.

The text your students practice rereading orally should also be relatively short--probably 50-200 words, depending on the age of the students. You should also use a variety of reading materials, including stories, nonfiction, and poetry. Poetry is especially well suited to fluency practice because poems for children are often short and they contain rhythm, rhyme, and meaning, making practice easy, fun, and rewarding.

How to have your students read aloud repeatedly. There are several ways that your students can practice orally rereading text, including student-adult reading, choral (or unison) reading, tape-assisted reading, partner reading, and readers' theatre.

Student-adult reading. In student-adult reading, the student reads one-on-one with an adult. The adult can be you, a parent, a classroom aide, or a tutor. The adult reads the text first, providing the students with a model of fluent reading. Then the student reads the same passage to the adult with the adult providing assistance and encouragement. The student rereads the passage until the reading is quite fluent. This should take approximately three to four rereading.

Choral reading. In choral, or unison, reading, students read along as a group with you (or another fluent adult reader). Of course, to do so, students must be able to see the same text that you are reading. They might follow along as you read from a big book, or they might read from their own copy of the book you are reading. For choral reading, choose a book that is not too long and that you think is at the independent reading level of most students. Patterned or predictable books are particularly useful for choral reading, because their repetitious style invites students to join in. Begin by reading the book aloud as you model fluent reading.

Then reread the book and invite students to join in as they recognize the words you are reading. Continue rereading the book, encouraging students to read along as they are able. Students should read the book with you three to five time's total (though not necessarily on the same day). At this time, students should be able to read the text independently.

Tape-assisted reading. In tape-assisted reading, students read along in their books as they hear a fluent reader read the book on an audiotape. For tape-assisted reading, you need a book at a student's independent reading level and a tape recording of the book read by a fluent reader at about 80+100 words per minute. The tape should not have sound effects or music. For the first reading, the student should follow along with the tape, pointing to each word in her or his book as the reader reads it. Next, the student should try to read aloud along with the tape. Reading along with the tape should continue until the student is able to read the book independently, without the support of the tape.

Partner reading. In partner reading, paired students take turns reading aloud to each other. For partner reading, more fluent readers can be paired with less fluent readers. The stronger reader reads a paragraph or page first, providing a model of fluent reading. Then the less fluent reader reads the same text aloud. The stronger student gives help with word recognition and provides feedback and encouragement to the less fluent partner. The less fluent partner rereads the passage until he or she can read it independently. Partner reading need not be done with a more and less fluent reader. In another form of partner reading, children who read at the same level are paired to reread a story that they have received instruction on during a teacher-guided part of the lesson. Two readers of equal ability can practice rereading after hearing the teacher read the passage.

Readers' theatre. In readers' theatre, students rehearse and perform a play for peers or others. They read from scripts that have been derived from books that are rich in dialogue. Students play characters who speak lines or a narrator who shares necessary background information. Readers' theatre provides readers with a legitimate reason to reread text and to practice fluency. Readers' theatre also promotes cooperative interaction with peers and makes the reading task appealing.

Activities For Repeated Oral Reading Practice

Student-adult reading--reading one-on-one with an adult, who provides a model of fluent reading, helps with word recognition, and provides feedback.

Choral reading--reading aloud simultaneously in a group.

Tape-assisted reading--reading aloud simultaneously or as an echo with an audio-taped model.

Partner reading--reading aloud with a more fluent partner (or with a partner of equal ability) who provides a model of fluent reading, helps with word recognition, and provides feedback.

Readers' theatre--the rehearsing and performing before an audience of a dialogue-rich script derived from a book.

Procedure For Calculating Words Correct Per Minute

One-minute reading: Total words read-errors = words correct per minute

- Select two or three brief passages from a grade- level basal text or other grade-level material (regardless of students' instructional levels).

- Have individual students read each passage aloud for exactly one minute.
- Count the total number of words the student read for each passage. Compute the average number of words read per minute.
- Count the number of errors the student made on each passage. Compute the average number of errors per minute.
- Subtract the average number of errors read per minute from the average total number of words read per minute. The result is the average number of words correct per minute (WCPM).
- Repeat the procedure several times during the year. Graphing students' WCPM throughout the year easily captures their reading growth.
- Compare the results with published norms or standards to determine whether students are making suitable progress in their fluency. For example, according to one published norm, students should be reading approximately 60 words per minute correctly by the end of first grade, 90-100 words per minute correctly by the end of second grade, and approximately 114 words per minute correctly by the end of third grade.

What Should I Do About Silent, Independent Reading In The Classroom?

Reading fluency growth is greatest when students are working directly with you. Therefore, you should use most of your allocated reading instruction time for direct teaching of reading skills and strategies. Although silent, independent reading may be a way to increase fluency and reading achievement, it should not be used in place of direct instruction in reading.

Direct instruction is especially important for readers who are struggling. Readers who have not yet attained fluency are not likely to make effective and efficient use of silent, independent reading time. For these students, independent reading takes time away from needed reading instruction.

Rather than allocating instructional time for independent reading in the classroom, encourage your students to read more outside of school. They can read with an adult or other family member. Or, they can read on their own with books at their independent reading level. Of course, students might also read on their own during independent work time in the classroom--for example, as another small group is receiving reading instruction, or after they have completed one activity and are waiting for a new activity to begin.

When Should Fluency Instruction Begin? When Should It End?

Fluency instruction is useful when students are not automatic at recognizing the words in their texts. How can you tell when students are not automatic? There is a strong indication that a student needs fluency instruction:

- if you ask the student to read orally from a text that he or she has not practiced; and the student makes more than ten percent word recognition errors;

- if the student cannot read orally with expression; or
- if the student's comprehension is poor for the text that she or he reads orally.

Is increasing word recognition skills sufficient for developing fluency?

Isolated word recognition is a necessary but not sufficient condition for fluent reading. Throughout much of the twentieth century, it was widely assumed that fluency was the result of word recognition proficiency. Instruction, therefore, focused primarily on the development of word recognition. In recent years, however, research has shown that fluency is a separate component of reading that can be developed through instruction. Having students review and rehearse word lists (for example, by using flash cards) may improve their ability to recognize the words in isolation, but this ability may not transfer to words presented in actual texts. Developing reading fluency in texts must be developed systematically.

Should I assess fluency? If so, how?

You should formally and informally assess fluency regularly to ensure that your students are making appropriate progress. The most informal assessment is simply listening to students read aloud and making a judgment about their progress in fluency. You should, however, also include more formal measures of fluency. For example, the student's reading rate should be faster than 90 words a minute, the student should be able to read orally with expression, and the student should be able to comprehend what is read while reading orally. Probably the easiest way to formally assess fluency is to take timed samples of students' reading and to compare their performance (number of words read correctly per minute) with published oral reading fluency norms or standards. Monitoring your students' progress in reading fluency will help you determine the effectiveness of your instruction and set instructional goals. Also, seeing their fluency growth reflected in the graphs you keep can motivate students. Other procedures that have been used for measuring fluency include Informal Reading Inventories (IRIs), miscue analysis, and running records. The purpose of these procedures, however, is to identify the kinds of word recognition problems students may have, not to measure fluency. Also, these procedures are quite time-consuming. Simpler measures of speed and accuracy, such as calculating words read correctly per minute are more appropriate for monitoring fluency.

Reading fluency encompasses the speed or rate of reading, as well as the ability to read materials with expression. Meyer & Felton (1999) defined fluency as "the ability to read connected text rapid, smoothly, effortlessly, and automatically with little conscious attention to the mechanics of reading, such as decoding" (1999, p. 284). Children are successful with decoding when the process used to identify words is fast and nearly effortless or automatic. As noted, the concept of automaticity refers to a student's ability to recognize words rapidly with little attention required to the word's appearance. The ability to read words by sight automatically is the key to skilled reading (Goldstein 2001).

Some children have developed accurate word pronunciation skills but read slowly. For these children, decoding is not automatic or fluent, and their limited fluency may affect performance in the following ways: 1) they read less text than peers and have less time to remember, review, or comprehend the text; 2) they expend more cognitive energy than peers trying to identify individual words; and 3) they may be less able to retain text in their memories and less likely to integrate those segments with other parts of the text (Mastropieri, Leinart, & Scruggs, 1999).

Determining A Student's Reading Rate

A student's reading rate may be calculated by dividing the number of words read correctly by the total amount of reading time. You may count out 100 words in a passage and then time the student as he or she reads the passage. Carver (1990).

Adjusting Reading Rate

Most people have a constant rate when reading. This rate is the fastest pace at which a person can understand complete thoughts in successive sentences of relatively easy material. As long as the material is relatively easy to read, a person's rate stays constant. For different types of tasks, however, readers often alter their rate. Students with slow reading rates are often not aware that good readers adjust their rate depending on the purpose of reading. Making these types of adjustments is particularly important for studying or completing assigned readings because a student with poor reading skills otherwise struggles to complete lengthy reading assignments.

Average rates for reading with understanding for students in Grades 2-12

Grade equivalent	Standard words per minute
2.5	121
3.5	135
4.5	149
5.5	163
6.5	177
7.5	191
8.5	205
9.5	219
10.5	233
11.5	247
12.5	261

Source: Carver (1990). A standard word is six letter spaces including punctuation and spacing.

Carver (1990) used the analogy of adjusting reading speed to the shifting of gears in a car. First and second gears are the slowest, most powerful gears. First gear is used to memorize materials. Second gear is used to learn material. Third gear is the typical reading rate. The fourth gear, skimming, and the fifth gear, scanning, are the fastest but least powerful gears. These gears are useful when you are trying to locate a specific piece of information or trying to get the general sense of a passage without reading every word.

As an adult reader, consider the ways that you monitor your reading pace and shift gears depending on your goals. If you are trying to memorize material for a test, your pace is slow and reflective, characterized by stopping and reviewing as you progress. If you are reading a novel for pleasure, your pace is steady and fluent. If you are searching for information in a catalog, your pace is rapid. As a skilled reader, you know how to adjust the gears of your reading on the basis of your purpose.

Some children have not learned how to adjust their reading rates. They attempt to read information in an encyclopedia at the same pace that they read a novel. To help develop increased reading speed, encourage students to adjust their rate depending on the purpose of reading. Provide practice in skimming through a chapter to get a sense of the information and then how to study that chapter for the weekly test. Demonstrate to students how you change your rate for different types of reading materials.

Activities for Increasing Reading Rate

Students who would benefit from methods to increase reading speed are often described by their teachers as slow, laborious readers who read word-by-word with limited expression. These types of techniques are most useful with students who have acquired some proficiency in decoding skill but whose level of decoding skill is lower than their oral language abilities. Methods for increasing reading rate have several common features: 1) students listen to text as they follow along with the book, 2) students follow the print using their fingers as guides, and 3) reading materials are used that students would be unable to read independently. Chard and Osborn (1999a) suggested that a beginning reading program should provide opportunities for partner reading, practice reading difficult words prior to reading the text, timings for accuracy and rate, opportunities to hear books read, and opportunities to read to others. The following methods are easy to use.

Speed Drills

For reading lists of words with a speed drill and a 1-minute timing, Fischer (1999) suggested using the following general guidelines: 30 correct wpm for first- and second-grade children; 40 correct wpm for third-grade children; 60 correct wpm for mid-third-grade; and 80 wpm for students in fourth grade and higher. To conduct a speed drill, have the student read a list of words for 1 minute as you record the number of errors. You may use a high-frequency word list or the sample speed drills provided in Fischer's program Concept Phonics (see Additional Resources). These drills are designed to develop automatic sight recognition of words.

Rapid Word Recognition Chart

A way to improve speed of recognition for words with an irregular element is the use of a rapid word recognition chart (Carreker, 1999). The chart is similar to a rapid serial-naming task. It is a matrix that contains five rows of six exception words (e.g., who and said), with each row containing the same six words in a different order. After a brief review of the words, students are timed for 1 minute as they read the words in the squares aloud. Students can then count and record the number of words read correctly. This type of procedure can help students like Ben who struggle to memorize words with irregular orthographic patterns.

Chapter VI

Vocabulary Instruction

Word knowledge has particular importance in literate societies. It contributes significantly to achievement in the subjects of the school curriculum, as well as in formal and informal speaking and writing. Most people feel that there is a common sense relationship between vocabulary and comprehension--messages are composed of ideas, and ideas are expressed in words. Most theorists and researchers in education have assumed that vocabulary knowledge and reading comprehension are closely related, and numerous studies have shown the strong correlation between the two (Baker, 1995; Nagy, 1988; Nelson-Herber, 1986).

Although the opportunities for vocabulary instruction are especially pronounced in language arts and reading, vocabulary instruction properly belongs in all subjects of the curriculum in which learners meet both new ideas and the words by which they are represented in the language. This Digest will consider several viewpoints on teaching vocabulary, offer some strategies for implementing vocabulary teaching, and suggest some sources for further reading.

Teacher's dilemma

From a teacher's point of view the issue in the classroom usually revolves around how to improve the student's reading comprehension, whether it is in content area reading or in the language arts. Should the teacher teach vocabulary directly or incidentally? That is, should words be targeted for the learners or should they develop naturally through reading and the learner's desire to clarify concepts? Evidence falls in both directions. Certainly vocabulary knowledge can be acquired through reading and discussions about certain contexts (Nagy et al, 1985). But it appears that direct instruction is more effective than incidental learning for the acquisition of a particular vocabulary, and also more efficient (McKeown and Beck, 1988). However, in one study of fourth graders that examined whether a context or a definitional approach was better for vocabulary development, Szymborski (1995) found that there was no significant difference in raw scores between the samples using the two different approaches.

Instructional techniques

It is generally accepted that students learn vocabulary more effectively when they are directly involved in constructing meaning rather than in memorizing definitions or synonyms. Thus, techniques such as webbing that involve students' own perspectives in creating interactions that gradually clarify targeted vocabulary may be a way to combine direct teaching and incidental learning in one exercise. Teachers can use students' personal experiences to develop vocabulary in the classroom. Through informal activities such as semantic association students brainstorm a list of words associated with a familiar word, pooling their knowledge of pertinent vocabulary as they discuss the less familiar words on the list. Semantic mapping goes a step further, grouping the words on the list into categories and arranging them on the visual "map" so that relationships among the words become clearer. In semantic feature analysis, words are grouped according to certain features, usually with the aid of a chart that graphically depicts similarities and differences among features of different words. Finally, analogies are a useful way of encouraging thoughtful discussion about relationships among meanings of words.

Content Area Reading

In content area reading, the development of vocabulary as a study of relationships seems particularly pertinent. Recognition of isolated information in an article on mechanization, for instance, may represent little understanding of the changes that are occurring as industry moves from human labor to robotics. Barton and Calfee (1989) suggest using a vocabulary matrix to establish the dimensions of a subject. The power of any vocabulary matrix lies in its image of connected ideas, in its process of discovering context for a new word, and in its visual reminder of gaps in our understanding.

Vocabulary development in any subject can proceed by asking students to reveal any vocabulary framework that they already have. Those known words may help them associate meaning with new vocabulary. In that way, definitions and the particular meaning within a given sentence have a context and a set of relations to build on.

One group technique that enables students to list synonyms and/or definitional phrases that they already associate with the topic involves the construction of a simple T-bar chart. Suppose, for example, an article on protecting the environment includes the word "menace." The teacher lists words that students associate with threats to the environment. Associated terms and synonyms are then listed in the T-bar chart.

With this kind of visual representation of a word and related terms, a matrix is begun for most students and the definition is enriched. The semantic context may now be rich enough for the reader to use this word in its context (Moore et al, 1989). To build background and to understand vocabulary in content area reading, students need the benefit of seeing multiple relationships.

Teaching Vocabulary

Christen and Murphy (1991) contend that research clearly emphasizes that for learning to occur, new information must be integrated with what the learner already knows. They feel that teaching vocabulary as a prereading step is an instructional intervention that should be considered when readers lack the prior or background knowledge to read in a content area. Kueker (1990) also argues that prereading activities help enormously in reading comprehension.

Another technique to help students see a word in a broader context is to have them answers the following questions: (1) what is it? (2) what is it like?; (3) what are some examples? Schwartz and Raphael (1985) believe that this list of 3 questions helps students see relationships between familiar and less familiar terms and also brings the meaning of an unknown term into focus by requiring analogies and examples.

LANGUAGE ARTS

In facilitating vocabulary instruction in the language arts classroom, Hodapp and Hodapp (1996) suggest using vocabulary packs and cued spelling as intervention strategies, while Cooter (1991) discusses using storytelling. Wilkinson (1994) opts for enlivening vocabulary lessons by combining them with two effective teaching strategies--cooperative learning and story development by students. Ruddiman (1993) also offers activities for vocabulary development. Bear et al (1996) presents a practical way for teachers to study words with students, providing more than 300 word study activities which are set up to follow literacy development from emergent to more mature, specialized stages (Baker & Scott, 1995).

In the language arts classroom, the role of writing is an integral part of reading instruction and offers a means for readers to extend and clarify their ideas. Students need many opportunities to write each day. Through writing workshops, students learn specific writing strategies and produce their own authentic writings. It is important that students at all grade levels write a range of pieces, including narrative, persuasive, informational, fiction, and poetry. In addition, there should be a seamless integration of word processing activities into a program of reading and writing instruction (Indiana Department of Education. (2000).

Language arts literacy capture language experiences all children need in order to grow intellectually, socially, and emotionally in classrooms across the curriculum. The standards are intended to promote students' capacities to construct meaning in any arena, with others as well as on their own. If students learn to read, write, speak, listen, and view critically, strategically, and creatively, and if they learn to use these arts individually and with others, they will have the literacy skills they need to discover personal and shared meaning throughout their lives.

The language arts are integrative, interactive ways of communicating that develop through reading, writing, speaking, listening, and viewing. They are the means through which one is able to receive information; think logically and creatively; express ideas; understand and participate meaningfully in spoken, written, and nonverbal communications; formulate and answer questions; and search for, organize, evaluate, and apply information. Literacy is a way to acquire knowledge for thinking and communicating; it is more than the acquisition of a specific, predetermined set of skills in reading, writing, speaking, listening, and viewing. Literacy is also recognizing and understanding one's own purposes for thinking and communicating (through print or nonprinting, verbal or nonverbal means) and being able to use one's own resources to achieve those purposes.

Underlying the standards for language arts literacy are four assumptions about language learning. First, language is an active process for constructing meaning. Even the quiet listener is actively working to link prior knowledge and understanding to what other people say. Second, language develops in a social context. While language is used in private activities, the use of language almost always relates to others. Each of us is an active audience for those who create spoken, written, or visual texts; others listen to our thoughts and read our writing. Third, language ability increases in complexity if language is used in increasingly complex ways. Language learners must engage in texts and conversations that are rich in ideas and increasingly complex in the patterns of language they display. Finally, learners achieve mastery of language arts literacy not by adding skills one-by-one to their repertoire, but rather by using and exploring language in its many dimensions.

Although the standards define five separate strands of the language arts, these arts are integrative and meant to work together to inform and enrich each other. The language arts are interdependent processes that often merge in an integrated act of rehearsal, reflection, and learning. The division of language arts into separate standards and lettered strands is merely a method that allows us to highlight the special features of each and to identify developmentally appropriate skills and behaviors among language arts learners. The separation is not meant to suggest hierarchical order or any linear or sequential approach to literacy instruction. The standards are not intended to be a curriculum guide but should be used as a catalyst for curriculum alignment and renewal. They are the foundation for the universal thinking skills and strategies that enable all learners to contribute effectively to a global society.

The standards represent the importance of language arts to learning in two distinct but complementary ways. On the one hand, students develop the skills they will carry with them into adulthood as contributing members of society: critical thinking, problem solving, and creativity. On the other hand, students discover the inner joy and self-illumination that come with reading great literature and communicating through speech and writing. These two views are complementary; in striving for the goals of one, the goals of the other are fostered.

STATE READING GOAL

A primary goal of all states is that **"Students will read well and independently by the end of the third grade."** In order to accomplish this goal, the language arts committee has placed a strong emphasis on developing performance benchmarks in grades K-12 that reflect both a state and national perspective on reading achievement. Teachers and parents can assist students in achieving these proficiencies by recognizing that learning extends beyond the classroom door to everyday experiences related to self, others, and the world.

The following set of beliefs about students, teaching, and the language arts learning process were established as the underlying framework for standards revisions. A "balanced and comprehensive approach" to instruction is essential in all language arts programs, and classrooms should provide students with:

- Differentiated instructional strategies to address individual learning styles and diverse student needs;
- Exposure to and experience with many literary genres through reaction, reflection, and introspection;
- Instructional skills and strategies, including direct and explicit instruction; modeling of skills/strategies for students, and opportunities for students to be a teacher to others, that ready students to become competent readers, writers, speakers, listeners, and viewers;
- Instruction delivered in meaningful contexts so that students preserve the learning for future use or transfer to other learning;
- "Active learning" in which students are engaged in active questioning, active listening, authentic activities, and the learning process;
- Explicit teaching of skills as a means of supporting mastery of standard English conventions, comprehension strategies, and communication skills;
- Acquisition of reading and literacy skills in all content areas to support learning;
- Development of self-help strategies that are practiced across all disciplines;
- Connections to prior knowledge as a necessary component of new learning and retention;
- Immersion in reading, writing, listening, speaking, and viewing strands that leads to deeper and wider understanding;
- Use of textual resources, especially those linked to current technologies, as an integral part of a language arts literacy program;
- Experiences using technology as a tool for learning, especially as it applies to research and data retrieval;
- Time to practice learned skills and reflect on one's work as an important part of the learning process;
- Activities encouraging problem-solving and inquiry skills as critical attributes to learning; and
- Explicit and systematic instruction in phonics and phonemic awareness, fluency, comprehension, and vocabulary development.

Yvonne L. Simon

The language arts classroom should be purposeful, stimulating to the senses, and engaging for all types of learners, including varied activities for visual, auditory, and kinesthetic learners. Classroom organization should include some form of team and partner work and provide an environment that is responsive to students' personal and academic goals.

Brain research clearly shows implications for student learning when there are links to the arts, like classical music, and the real world. For example, having young children recite the alphabet with a song enables the learner to remember and retain the information longer. Language arts classrooms should be alive with authentic learning opportunities that motivate and incorporate the arts.

Mastering the first 1,200 words (up to Level 120) gives students the minimum vocabulary skills needed to comprehend test questions and answers in order to pass the Reading Test with a "LEVEL 2" score. Spending time on Study Guides and Practice Tests is time wasted if students have not first mastered the minimum vocabulary needed to read test questions fluently. This is why we have developed the vocabulary list. Words have been divided into 120 Levels with 10 words per "Level." To increase the efficiency of the test vocabulary, words have been organized from the most common at the beginning to the least common words toward the end of the list. Therefore, the words at the beginning appear on the test more frequently than the words at the end. Brevard County's Testing/Assessment Division states that recent assessments of students who "*just miss*" passing the test show they are typically reading at approximately late 2nd to beginning 3rd grade level. Beginning 3rd grade level on our Vocabulary List is approximately Levels 110-120. Therefore, for students to have any chance of passing the FCAT, they need to have mastered at least Levels 1- 120 and preferably higher.

Level 118 row - (2 sounds)	Level 119 short a	Level 120 short a
1. row	1. Act	1. Gas
2. bow	2. Tag	2. Sack
3. window	3. Lamp	3. Tan
4. fellow	4. Rack	4. Slap
5. town	5. Pack	5. Map
6. clown	6. Glad	6. Trap
7. crown	7. Lamb	7. Tank
8. flower	8. Wrap	8. Lack
9. prove	9. Fry	9. Ocean
10. garage	10. Cough	

Level 121	Level 122 Short i	Level 123 Final e-rule
1. Net	1. Rid	1. pile
2. Hen	2. brick	2. rope
3. Mend	3. Pin	3. shine
4. swept	4. Spin	4. kite
5. Rent	5. Gift	5. hose
6. Melt	6. Hill	6. case
7. Fled	7. Rich	7. dove
8. Shell	8. Whip	8. waste
9. Judge	9. route	9. iron
10. capital	10. monkey	10. honor

Level 124 ai-ea	Level 125 ny-ly-ry	Level 126 2 consonant rule
1. Tail	1. Tiny	1. offer
2. Sail	2. Ugly	2. basket
3. Nail	3. Silly	3. grandmother
4. Afraid	4. Worry	4. grandfather
5. Leaf	5. Jelly	5. pocket
6. Tease	6. Cherry	6. pillow
7. Dream	7. Library	7. member
8. breathe	8. Lonely	8. grandpa
9. Heart	9. Soup	9. deny
10. proper	10. Bushel	10. engine

Level 127 ar-er	Level 128 Final e-rule	Level 129 c rule-ou
1. Arm	1. bone	1. mice
2. March	2. file	2. office
3. Charm	3. scare	3. circus
4. Charge	4. airplane	4. notice
5. Farmer	5. wave	5. mouse
6. Skirt	6. wife	6. wound
7. Church	7. tire	7. mountain
8. Enter	8. strange	8. surround
9. Ache	9. honey	9. piano
10. Mirror	10. proper	10. court

Level 130 Short a	Level 131 Short e- short i	Level 132 Short o-short u
1. Tax	1. shed	1. boss
2. Pat	2. shelf	2. fond
3. Rat	3. chest	3. lock
4. Blank	4. stretch	4. block
5. Band	5. bid	5. tub
6. Sand	6. dim	6. buzz
7. Calf	7. ditch	7. rush
8. backwards	8. grip	8. thus
9. Ghost	9. broad	9. chalk
10. Character	10. apron	10. machine

Level 133 Final e-rule		Level 134 ai		Level 135 ea (long sound)	
1.	eve	1.	air	1.	bead
2.	froze	2.	main	2.	bean
3.	frame	3.	grain	3.	deal
4.	prize	4.	daisy	4.	cream
5.	cave	5.	pair	5.	heap
6.	brave	6.	plain	6.	feast
7.	fare	7.	remain	7.	leaves
8.	continue	8.	contain	8.	disappear
9.	oven	9.	model	9.	worm
10.	search	10.	compare	10.	magazine

Level 136 my-dy-ry-cy-ty	Level 137 1 consonant rule	Level 138 2 consonant rule
1. Army	1. fever	1. kitten
2. Muddy	2. frozen	2. supper
3. Fairy	3. grapes	3. officer
4. Marry	4. useless	4. sandwich
5. Fancy	5. silent	5. bitter
6. History	6. silence	6. supply
7. Century	7. remind	7. scissors
8. Electricity	8. review	8. language
9. Record	9. zero	9. shove
10. Experience	10. guard	10. travel

Level 139 er-or	Level 140 le-ow	Level 141 ing-oo
1. eraser	1. kettle	1. king
2. drawer	2. jungle	2. Wing
3. prayer	3. handle	3. Dying
4. wonder	4. gentle	4. Spring
5. form	5. crow	5. Zoo
6. bore	6. arrow	6. Tool
7. cord	7. power	7. Proof
8. corn	8. allow	8. Bloom
9. shovel	9. bear	9. Glove
10. arrest	10. bandage	10. Chemical

Level 142 Short a	Level 143 Short I- - short u	Level 144 Final e-rule
1. mat	1. pig	1. cane
2. camp	2. tin	2. cape
3. match	3. ship	3. cage
4. branch	4. pitch	4. figure
5. damp	5. gum	5. hike
6. glass	6. gun	6. wipe
7. blanket	7. nut	7. stare
8. fasten	8. hunt	8. wire
9. system	9. flood	9. grind
10. tomato	10. respect	10. ought

Level 145 ai-ee		Level 146 ea		Level 147 ee	
1.	aim	1.	tea	1.	beet
2.	gain	2.	tear	2.	weed
3.	fail	3.	peas	3.	cheese
4.	paint	4.	beach	4.	squeeze
5.	seed	5.	pear	5.	weed
6.	beef	6.	breast	6.	seek
7.	peep	7.	heaven	7.	sheet
8.	speed	8.	health	8.	freedom
9.	solid	9.	wolf	9.	dodge
10.	gasoline	10.	errand	10.	pledge

Level 48 Final e-rule	Level 149 oa-ar	Level 150 or-ir-ur
1. dine	1. soak	1. horn
2. dare	2. toad	2. forest
3. flame	3. coast	3. porch
4. invite	4. board	4. nor
5. cute	5. star	5. birth
6. cure	6. garden	6. turkey
7. knife	7. carpet	7. surface
8. provide	8. market	8. squirrel
9. rye	9. bull	9. rapid
10. soldier	10. bullet	10. tobacco

Level 151 C-rule-au	Level 152 Final e-rule	Level 153 tion-ture
1. rice	1. ripe	1. motion
2. science	2. rose	2. station
3. force	3. bare	3. vacation
4. citizen	4. sunshine	4. position
5. snow	5. scale	5. nature
6. narrow	6. snake	6. capture
7. owl	7. produce	7. furniture
8. towel	8. refuse	8. adventure
9. thief	9. hoe	9. melon
10. priest	10. butcher	10. niece

Level 154 oo-ou	Level 155 Short vowel mix	Level 156 Final e-rule
1. roof	1. log	1. pipe
2. foolish	2. tent	2. smoke
3. woolen	3. mud	3. scene
4. scooter	4. split	4. spare
5. proud	5. bud	5. pave
6. bound	6. chop	6. stove
7. outfit	7. drill	7. paste
8. county	8. sled	8. trade
9. blind	9. chief	9. canoe
10. graduate	10. sleigh	10. reply

Level 157
ea

1. Seal
2. Peach
3. Stream
4. Wheat
5. Steam
6. Spear
7. Grease
8. Preach
9. Stalk
10. Medicine

Level 158
ee

1. deer
2. creek
3. freeze
4. cheep
5. steer
6. sleeve
7. steel
8. queen
9. lion
10. freight

Level 159
ry-vy-ny-ty-my-ly

1. navy
2. berry
3. jolly
4. factory
5. pony
6. duty
7. enemy
8. company
9. colt
10. elephant

Vocabulary is a set of words known to a person or other entity, or that are part of a specific language.

The vocabulary of a person is defined either as the set of all words that are understood by that person or the set of all words likely to be used by that person when constructing new sentences. So "curse" is a regular part of the vocabulary of native English speakers but "imprecate" is not, even though the two words are synonyms. The richness of a person's vocabulary is popularly thought to be a reflection of intelligence or level of education. Accordingly, many standardized tests, such as the SAT, have questions that test vocabulary.

Increasing the size of one's vocabulary, also called *vocabulary building,* is generally considered to be an important part of both learning a language and improving one's skills in a language in which one is already proficient. Hence schoolchildren are often taught new words as a part of a particular unit or lesson. Similarly, many adults find vocabulary building to be a fun and educational activity, as evidenced in the popularity of "word-a-day" services such as mailing lists and desktop calendars.

The word "vocabulary" is also used figuratively for qualities or techniques distinctive to a particular style, especially an architectural style. Many teachers help students expand their vocabulary by assigning packets to be done weekly.

According to ***Jean Aitchison***, the time to recognize a word may be less than 200 ms after onset; in many cases the word is already recognized before it has even ended. (***Shadowing*** and ***lexical decision tasks*** were used to determine this number.)Brain research has found that the brain is managing vocabulary through mental orthographic images (MOI), a database of visual imprints of words learned. Since the brain has the ability to quickly jump to conclusions as it hears words, it is to be expected that a similar database is storing sound impressions of words as well.

Mental orthographic *images* enable the mind to quickly skip through text, absorbing its content without actually deciphering words letter by letter. It seems that the educated mind makes writing decisions based on what "looks right" and reading decisions based on what "looks like", allowing for rapid processing.

Elaborating Vocabulary Instruction

When you think of vocabulary, there is a good chance that you think of long lists of words from social studies or science textbooks, spelling word lists, or even the humongous lists of terms to study for college entrance exams. Zillions of flash cards also may come to mind. No doubt you share the common childhood experience of having to "go look up the words in a dictionary, write the definition, and then write a sentence using the term" -- but how much of that vocabulary do you remember now? Do you remember how you could rote copy the definition of a term as part of a homework assignment, but have no real idea what the definition meant and still get an 'A' on the assignment? (Ellis, 2002)

Perhaps the least effective way to study vocabulary is the "look and remember" technique. Here, students typically stare at the term and definition, apparently trying to activate photographic memory they wish they had. Another common study technique is 'rote verbal rehearsal' -- saying the word over and over again, usually in the exact language and format from which the definition originally came.

Ross Perot, with his unique use of the English language, said it best "That dog don't hunt!" In other words, many of the traditional techniques teachers and students use to learn vocabulary does not work because most students, not just those with learning problems, rarely remember the meanings of new terms beyond the test. This raises a very disconcerting question: If students don't remember the definitions of new terms after the test, why bother requiring them to memorize these definitions in the first place since it seems to be a waste of time?

We know from research that new terms must be defined using language and examples which are already familiar to students, and that the more ideas from background knowledge with which the student can associate the new term, the more likely it will become well 'networked' and permanent part of memory. There are a variety of tactics and strategies that can be mediated by the teacher to help students understand and remember new terms as well as the significance of important names, events, places, or processes. All of these tactics involve facilitating elaboration in various ways.

Elaborating Definitions of New Terms

There are several elaboration techniques that appear to be particularly powerful facilitators of comprehension and memory of new terms. These are briefly described below.

Elaboration Technique #1:

Teach new terms in context of a meaningful subject-matter lesson, and facilitate student discussion that centers on use of the new term. At some point, students should use the new term themselves in a sentence within the context of discussing broader topics.

The traditional practice of having students look up definitions and then write sentences using the new terms likely stems from the idea that students must think of the term and create a context for which it might be appropriately used. While composing written sentences clearly is an important elaboration technique for the learner, essential to also include in the learning process is learning about the term within an overall context so that relational understanding can develop.

Although providing opportunities for students to elaborate about new terms requires a significant portion of class time, it is clearly a worthwhile instructional practice. The problem is, students are often expected to memorize the definitions of far more terms than there is time in class to elaborate upon. To provide meaningful opportunities for elaboration, we need to teach considerably fewer terms, and invest considerable more time in developing deep knowledge structures of those that are really essential for students to know. This means that students are typically expected to memorize far too many terms each week. The adage 'less is more depth' is more' is very true in this context.

Another implication of this first elaboration technique is that the common practice (often associated with language arts classes) of having students attempt to learn long lists of un-associated words without the benefit of learning them within some meaningful context is largely a waste of the teacher's and student's time. Figure 1 provides a set of guidelines for how to be more selective about deciding which terms students should be taught.

Guidelines for selecting to-be-learned vocabulary

Do...	Avoid...
Less is more -- depth is more. Teach fewer vocabulary terms, but teach them in a manner that results in deep understandings of each term.	Teaching or assigning words from textbooks just because they are highlighted in some way (italicized, bold face print, etc.).
Teach terms that are central to the unit or theme of study. These are terms that are so important that if the student does not understand them, s/he likely will have difficulty understanding the remainder of the unit.	Teaching or assigning words just because they appear in a list at the end of a text chapter.
Teach terms that address key concepts or ideas. While a text chapter may contain 15-20 vocabulary terms, there may be only 4 or 5 that address critical concepts in the chapter -- sometimes only 1 or 2!).	Teaching or assigning words that will have little utility once the student has passed the test.
Teach terms that will be used repeatedly throughout the semester. These are foundational concepts upon which a great deal of information will be built on over a long-term basis.	Assigning words the teacher cannot define.
	Assigning large quantities of words.
	Assigning words that students will rarely encounter again.

ELABORATION TECHNIQUE #2:

Facilitate paraphrasing of new term's definitions so that students can identify the core idea associated with the overall meaning of the term, as well as distinguish the new term's critical features. If you were to dissect the semantic structure of a new term, you would find that its definition actually has two main components: (i) The core idea of the new term is like its 'gist' or main idea; and (ii) critical features of the definition are specific bits of information in the definition that clarify the broader, more general core idea. This is analogous to paraphrasing main ideas of paragraphs when reading in which the reader says what the overall paragraph was about (main idea) and indicates important details in the paragraph. With new terms, the goal is to paraphrase the core idea of the term and identify specific critical-to-remember details that clarify the core idea.

ELABORATION TECHNIQUE #3:

Make background knowledge connections to the new term. While teaching the new term in context of a subject-matter lesson is a critical instructional technique, an equally important elaboration technique is for students to relate the term to something in which the students are already familiar. There is a wide array of methods by which students can formulate knowledge connections. For example, they can identify how the term is related to previous subject-matter they have learned, they can identify something from their personal life experiences the term reminds them of, they can create metaphors or similes for the term, or they can say how the term relates to understanding or solving some form of real-life problem. An essential part of this elaboration process is having the students explain the connection. For example, the students should not only say what personal experience the term makes them think of, but also why it reminds them of it.

ELABORATION TECHNIQUE #4:

Identify examples/applications as well as non-examples/non-applications related to the new term's meaning. Comprehension is greatly enhanced if the learner can accurately identify examples of the term or ways the new term can be appropriately applied within the context of discussing another context. For example, the term 'peaceful resistance' might be used when describing Martin Luther King's approach to solving racial discrimination problems.

You will likely find that students' comprehension of new terms becomes considerably more focused and refined if they can also identify examples of what the term is not about or inappropriate applications of the term's use. Having the student discuss of what the term is not an example, or other concept with which someone should not confuse it, can facilitate this.

Elaboration technique #5:

Create multiple formats for which students can elaborate on the meaning of new terms. Many teachers will utilize all of the above elaboration processes within the context of a class discussion, and yet some students still do not seem to 'get it.' This is because the manner in which elaboration was facilitated was all 'lip-ear', or verbal or listening, forms of instruction. Writing elaborations, even for those where scripting is a laborious process, creates an opportunity for greater reflection on the term's meaning. Other forms of elaboration involve use acting out via role-play the meanings of some terms or creating mnemonic pictures or stories that capture the essence of a new term's meaning.

The Clarifying Routine focuses on ways each of the above forms of elaboration can be facilitated. The teachers use an instructional tool, called a Clarifying Table, to facilitate these kinds of thinking behaviors. Figure 2 illustrates a Clarifying Table that was used in the context of an integrated unit with a "Titanic" theme.

While some teachers use the Clarifying Table to pre-teach vocabulary terms students will encounter in an up-coming lesson, I have been most successful using it as a way to 'anchor' the meanings of terms whose meanings were first explored within the context of a subject-matter lesson. To put this in perspective, I might briefly introduce the meaning of new terms at the beginning of a lesson, and then more thoroughly explore their meanings during the subject-matter lesson, and finally, use the Clarifying Table to solidify understanding of those terms that are really essential for students to learn.

Forms of 'DO' instruction

The teacher can use the Cue-Do-Review sequence when applying the Routine. I have found that the 'Do' component of this routine can be very effectively applied in four basic ways (see Figure 3) adapted from Anita Archer's characterization of scaffolded instruction: 'I do it' (model), 'We do it' (provide guided practice), and 'You do it' (independent practice). The teacher should always include a 'You all do it' phase before asking student to complete an activity individually.

'I do it' instruction

The purpose of the first phase of 'Do' instruction is to provide students with a precise model of a well-constructed Clarifying Table depicting information related to an essential new term students need to learn. The first time students are introduced to Clarifying Tables, the teacher usually provide them with one that have been completely constructed ahead of time, and just walk them through it in much the same manner that has been explained and depicted on a web or other pre-constructed graphic organizer. After explaining the information depicted on the Clarifying Table, the teacher should ask students what they like about the table and how well it helps them understand the meaning of a new term. The teacher typically does this twice before moving to the next phase, 'We do it.'

'We do it' instruction

During 'We do it' instruction, the teacher co-constructs the Clarifying Tables with students. Although the teacher may have constructed one for a new term prior to class as part of the planning process, so that the instruction will go smoothly. The teacher does not show students a completed version. Rather, the teacher first teaches the meaning of the new term in the context of a subject-matter lesson, and then provides students with blank copies of a Clarifying Table. Together, we (students and teacher), decide what ideas should be noted on the form. Thus, the whole class decides on what to note as the "Core Idea" for the new term, what to list as "Clarifiers," "Knowledge Connections," and so forth.

'We do it' forms of instruction continue through the year, thus I never really stop co-constructing Clarifying Tables with students. As students become more confident and competent at constructing these tables, however, my role tends to shift from being the person who frequently cues students what to do and helps them actually phrase ideas to note on the form to a role that is much more like a "guide-on-the-side."

'You All Do It' Instruction

Once it becomes evident to the teacher that most students understand the purpose of the Clarifying Table, and can construct them with little assistance from the teacher, the teacher can begin incorporating cooperative learning activities where students work in pairs or small teams to construct Clarifying Tables without my assistance. While it varies depending of the nature of the class, the teacher usually begin incorporating 'You all do it' activities after we, as a class, have constructed between five and ten Clarifying Tables. Naturally, the more familiar students are with the meaning of the new term, the easier it is for them to construct Clarifying Tables. Thus it is very important that the teacher do a great job teaching the new terms and meanings in the context of the subject-matter lesson before asking students to work together to construct a Clarifying Table. 'You all do it' activities allow students to have some support, but the nature of the support comes from peers rather than the teacher.

'You do it' instruction

The Clarifying Table is a versatile tool that teachers can use to teach the meanings for new terms, and students can use as a strategy for independently studying new terms. 'You do it' activities are designed to enable students to perform this task without assistance from others. An example would be requiring students to construct Clarifying Tables for five terms in lieu of requiring them to complete traditional study guides or answer the end-of-chapter textbook questions.

Assignments that require students to independently construct Clarifying Tables only occur, however, after a sufficient amount of scaffolded instruction has previously occurred. A very common mistake is to jump from providing an initial model (I do it) to requiring students to independently do it themselves (You do it) without the intermediate guided practice mediated by the teacher and by peers.

INTEGRATING THE CLARIFYING ROUTINE WITH OTHER LEARNING STRATEGIES

One of the ways that teachers can use the clarifying routine is to assign reading passages, and have students take notes on the Clarifying Table about the main ideas and details of the text in the tradition of the Paraphrasing Strategy. Teachers can also incorporated it as a note taking tool that students used during the context of exploring a subject-matter lesson. Additionally, teachers can also use the Clarifying Table as a form of 'think sheet' students used to plan their writing. Students would first complete a Clarifying Table about their topic, and then, when writing their essays, use the completed Clarifying Tables as a guide for organizing their ideas and ensuring they discussed meaningful information in their social studies and literature-related writing assignments.

Clarifying Tables are designed to facilitate the development of deep knowledge structures or in-depth and thorough understanding of terms. The LINCS strategy, on the other hand, is designed to create a mechanism for ready recall of definitions so that test-performance increases substantially. Used together, they can form a powerful synergy to improve learning performance (Ellis, 2002)

Almost always, there is room at the bottom of the "Knowledge Connections" section of the Clarifying Table to note a LINCing Story or picture. Thus, teachers who have been using LINCS need not discontinue its use in lieu of the Clarifying Routine. Both work well together.

Besides, the Clarifying Routine can be used to help students develop in depth understanding of key terms associated with a unit of study primarily because it incorporates powerful elaboration tactics. The Clarifying Table is best used after the meanings of new terms have been explored in the context of a subject-matter lesson. The Table can be constructed by the teacher and presented to students as the meaning of a term is explored, it can be co-constructed by the class and teacher, or co-constructed by peers. Eventually, the Clarifying Table can become a powerful substitute for traditional homework assignments as students use them independently. The Clarifying Routine can also be readily used in conjunction with other learning strategies to develop literacy skills, note-taking skills, as well as test-preparation skills.

Context clues are words and phrases in a sentence which help you reason out the meaning of an unfamiliar word. Oftentimes you can figure out the meanings of new or unfamiliar vocabulary by paying attention to the surrounding language. The table below gives the types of clues, signals and examples of each clue.

Type of Context Clue	Definition	Signals	Examples
Antonym or Contrast Clue	Phrases or words that indicate opposite	**but, in contrast, however, instead of, unlike, yet**	Unlike his *quiet and low key* family, Brad is *garrulous.*
Definition or Example Clue	Phrases or words that define or explain	**is defined as, means, the term, [a term in boldface or italics] set off with commas**	*Sedentary* individuals, people who are not very active, often have diminished health.
General Knowledge	The meaning is derived from the experience and background knowledge of the reader; "common sense" and logic.	**the information may be something basically familiar to you**	Lourdes is always sucking up to the boss, even in front of others. That *sycophant* just doesn't care what others think of her behavior.
Restatement or Synonym Clue	Another word or phrase with the same or a similar meaning is used.	**in other word, that is, also known as, sometimes called, or**	The *dromedary*, commonly called a camel, stores fat in its hump.

While some teachers use the Clarifying Table to pre-teach vocabulary terms students will encounter in up-coming lessons, that you the teacher should put in place, so that the students will be successful in using it, and it is a way to 'anchor' the meanings of terms whose meanings were first explored within the context of a subject-matter lesson. To put this in perspective, the teacher might briefly introduce the meaning of new terms at the beginning of a lesson, and then more thoroughly explore their meanings during the subject-matter lesson, and finally, use the Clarifying Table to solidify understanding of those terms that are really essential for students to learn. (Ellis, 2002)

WHY TEACH VOCABULARY?

Studies have shown that reading comprehension and vocabulary knowledge are strongly correlated, and researchers have found that word knowledge in primary school can predict how well students will be able to comprehend texts they read in high school. Limited vocabulary prevents students from comprehending a text. Poor readers often read less, because reading is difficult and frustrating for them (Biemiller, 2001). This means they don't read enough to improve their vocabularies, which could, in turn, help them comprehend more. This perpetuating cycle can mean that as students continue through middle schools and high school, the gap between good and poor readers grows wider.

Direct instruction in vocabulary can help apprehend this cycle. Good readers often acquire much of their vocabulary through wide independent reading, also known as incidental learning. However, explicit instruction can help students learn enough words to become better readers and hence acquire even more words. Direct vocabulary instruction is useful for students who have a limited reading vocabulary and little exposure to incidental vocabulary learning outside of school. The average student learns about 3,000 words a year, or six to eight words per day, a remarkable achievement! If students are taught new words at a rate of eight to ten words per week for 37 to 50 weeks, about 300 to 500 words per year can be taught through direct instruction. This leaves a large portion of words to be learned through independent reading which is essential to acquiring word knowledge.

Although the percentage of words learned through direct instruction may seem small, it is significant. Stahl, 1999 has pointed out that for students at the lower end of the vocabulary range, who learn perhaps 1,000 words a year, a gain of 300 words equals a 30 percent increase, and that for average students a gain of even 10 percent is educationally significant, especially if it is repeated year after year. Experts agree that a combination of direct instruction of word meanings, discussions about words and word parts, and encouragement of wide reading is the best way to help students develop vocabulary.

How Direct Instruction Can Help Students Who Start with Smaller Vocabularies

Students come to school with greatly varying vocabularies. Some will know thousands more word meanings than other students in your class. This occurs in part because of the differences in the number of new words students are exposed to in their homes and communities. Students who come from homes where spoken and written vocabularies are limited will know fewer words than students who come from homes where exposure to a wide range of vocabulary is common. Arriving in class with a small vocabulary does not predict failure; it only highlights the need for direct vocabulary instruction in the schools. If we are serious about "increasing standards" and bringing a greater proportion of school children to high levels of academic accomplishment, we cannot continue to leave vocabulary development to parents, chance, and highly motivated reading (Texas Reading Initiative, 2000).

The key to increasing vocabulary is exposure to new words, not an innate ability to learn from context. Experts emphasize that vocabulary development is an attainable goal. If students are given the opportunity to learn new words as well as effective instruction, most students can acquire vocabulary at rates that will improve their comprehension. This enables them to read increasingly challenging texts with fluency and better their chances for success in school and afterward.

What Should Direct Instruction Include?

Subsequently, how do we teach students to acquire words? According to Biemiller, 2001, effective vocabulary instruction should include the following three components:

1. definitional and contextual information about a word
2. multiple exposures to a word in different contexts
3. encouragement of students' active participation in their word learning'

Definition and Context

Traditionally, vocabulary instruction has focused on having students look up word meanings and memorize them. This teaching approach, however, provides only superficial and short-term learning of words. Students who simply memorize word meanings frequently have trouble applying the information in definitions and often make mistakes about the meanings. To know a word, students need to see it in context and learn how its meaning relates to the words around it. An approach that includes definition as well as context can generate a full and flexible knowledge of word meanings. When students are given several sentences that use a word in different ways, they begin to see how a word's meaning can change and shift depending on its context. For example, consider the changes in the word got, as it appears in the following sentences:

Jessica got a fever

Jessica got rich

Jessica got a flower from Jeffrey.

Jeffrey got in trouble.

Although in most of these examples got conveys the idea of receiving, the meaning is slightly different in each one. Students need to see words in different contexts in order to learn them thoroughly.

Repeat, Repeat, and Repeat

Students benefit from seeing the same word several times. Word meanings are accumulated gradually. A word that is encountered once has about a 10 percent chance of being learned from context. When students see a word repeatedly, they gather more and more information about it until they acquire an idea of what it means. The more exposure students have to a word, the more likely it is that they will be able to define, comprehend, and remember it; good vocabulary instruction builds repetition into the learning process, so that students can learn more words more quickly. Using and applying several examples of a word in different contexts reinforces word knowledge. In this millennium, educators are becoming increasingly aware of the benefits of a structured vocabulary curriculum. A certain amount of time should be set aside each week for vocabulary instruction. A planned approach ensures that vocabulary instruction is given the attention it deserves. Important words and techniques for learning words are taught systematically and in depth (Gunning, 2003, p. 236). Research studies have established that, even though children learn many words incidentally, they also need and profit from the direct teaching of vocabulary. It is important that teachers provide explicit and direct vocabulary instruction for all students (Vacca et al, 2001, p. 308).

YOU CAN DO IT! EMPHASIZING ACTIVE PROCESSING BY STUDENTS

Students remember words better when they connect new meanings to knowledge they already have. This type of active processing occurs when students work with words in some of the following ways:

- produce antonyms and synonyms
- rewrite definitions
- identify examples and non-examples of the word
- use more than one new word in a sentence
- create sentences that contain the new word
- create scenarios or stories in which the word is used
- create silly questions using the word

Each of the above activities reinforces definitional or contextual information about the word and gives students a chance to own the word for themselves. Group discussion of word meanings also helps students learn new vocabulary by having to actively participate in their own learning.

GENERAL STRATEGIES AND SPECIFIC TECHNIQUES FOR TEACHING VOCABULARY

Effective vocabulary development is a multifaceted process requesting a combination of direct instruction, discussion, and active encouragement of independent learning strategies. On their own and in the classroom, students draw on a variety of methods to learn the thousands of words they acquire each year. The following are some general strategies and specific techniques to keep in mind as you teach vocabulary.

1. ENCOURAGING WIDE READING

Getting your students to read more may be the most valuable thing you can do to improve their vocabulary. Although direct instruction plays a crucial part in vocabulary growth, most of the words your students learn will be acquired through incidental learning, as they read on their own. (Edwards, 2001) states that wide reading is the main avenue for students' word acquisition. For example: if over a school year, a fifth grade reads for an hour each day, five days a week in and out of school at a conservative rate of 150 words per minute, the student will encounter 2,250,000 words in the course of reading. If 2 to 5 percent of the words the student encounters are unknown words, he or she will encounter from 45,000 to 112,500 new words. It is a known fact that students learn between 5 and 10 percent of previously unknown words from a single reading. Using the lower number given above for unknown words encountered during the reading program, we see that a student would learn at least 2,250 new words from context each year.

To be truly beneficial, wide reading should include texts with varied levels of difficulty. Students reading at or below their current levels will not dramatically increase their vocabulary. When students read texts that consist primarily of unknown words, they usually become frustrated. To help them get the most out of incidental learning, they should read some books for fun and others for challenge. Motivating students to read can be a difficult task. Here are a few suggestions for making reading appealing to students at all ability levels:

Devote some class time to independent silent reading. This time may be Particularly helpful for students who have never done extensive reading For pleasure. Reading for a length of time in class will enable students to do this on their own outside of class.

Make a variety of books available in class and recommend books for students to find in the library and to read outside of class.

Promote social interactions related to reading. Setting a time for regular book discussion will motivate students to read more and help them understand their reading better.

Model the importance you place on reading by telling students about books you are reading. When students have silent reading time, read a book of your own to show that reading is a valuable activity that you enjoy, too.

Emphasizing Learning From Context

Most of the words acquired through incidental reading are learned through context. Students learn from context by making connections between the new word and the context in which it appears. They also learn words through repeated exposures, gaining more comprehension of a word's meanings and functions by seeing it several times in different contexts. Experts debate the effectiveness of teaching students how to use context clues. While some studies show that teaching students how to identify and use context clues is an effective technique for increasing vocabulary, other research suggests that learning words from context is an innate skill that all readers use. (Kuhn and Stahl, 1999) have found that children of all abilities learn at the same rate from context; that is, advanced readers are no more efficient at learning from context than less advanced readers, the advanced readers simply read more. All experts, however, stress that it is crucial to make students aware of the importance of using context clues as an essential tool in word acquisition. Here are some techniques for enhancing students' awareness of the importance of context clues;

Model basic strategies for using context clues when reading text.

Provide explanation of how, when, and why to use context to figure out word meanings.

Provide guided practice in using context.

Remind students to apply the skill when reading on their own.

You can also use activities such as the Word Wizard chart (Beck, et al.) to make students aware of learning words in context. As you discuss unfamiliar words in class, you can add them to the chart. If a student comes across the word again when reading and notes its context, his or her name goes up on the chart. You can provide students with periodic rewards for being Word Wizards (that is, contributing many words to the chart). Another way to emphasize the importance of learning from context is to have students rate their knowledge of a new word by using a checklist such as the following;

	Can define	Have seen /heard	Don't know
hierarchy			
enlargement			
constitute			
appurtenance			
alignment			
dilapidated			
digress			
prosecute			
synchronize			
verdant			

These checklists can also be used in group activities in class. You may want to have students keep these checklists together in a notebook along with a running list of words they come across that intrigue or interest them. Encouraging a general awareness of words as fun and interesting in themselves will help students pursue their own vocabulary development. Using context is an important skill that students will employ frequently. However, in learning when to use context clues, students also need to know when not to use this strategy. Since many texts do not signal the meanings of words explicitly, using context is not always the best way to derive the meaning of new words.

Using Prefixes, Suffixes, and Root

Vacca et al, (2003), have noted that the upper elementary grades are a good time to start teaching students how to use word parts to figure out the meanings of words. Information from prefixes, suffixes, and roots can help students learn and remember words; using word parts can be a particularly useful strategy in reading content area texts. For example, science texts often include words that use the same word parts repeatedly, such as bio- in biosphere, biology, biodegradable, bioluminescence, and biochemical. Knowing the "bio" means life can help students recognize these words in context and add to their comprehension of these words. This particular root will also help students learn words across content areas. For example, in language arts students will encounter words such as biography.)

You can begin to teach word part strategy by telling students that words can be composed of affixes, prefixes, and suffixes, and roots. Learning to break words into affixes, and roots will make some long words more manageable for students who may be intimidated by the length of words such as interdependent. Modeling how to break words into parts may be necessary. To do this, you can teach them to cover prefixes such as inter- in the word interdependent, and see if they recognize the rest of the word. Then you can have them cover the suffix –ent, leaving depend. Further, modeling and practice with adding and removing prefixes and suffixes such as un- and able will give students facility with breaking words down into parts.

In teaching word parts, you should stress how the parts function to affect word meaning. You may want to point out that prefixes such as un-, super-, anti-, mis-, and sub change the meanings of the roots they precede in predictable ways. Since prefixes are consistently defined, you may want to supply definitions of the prefixes given in the table below. Suffixes have less stable meanings, but learning to recognize common suffixes such as –tion, -less, -ed, and –ing will help students know a word's function For example,

The Most Frequent Affixes In Printed English

Rank	Prefix	% of All Prefixed Words	Suffix	% of All Suffixed Words
1	un-	26	-s, -es	31
2	re-	14	-ed	20

3	in-,im-,il-,ir-(not)	11	-ing	14
4	dis-	7	-ly	7
5	en-, em-	4	-er,-or (agent)	4
6	non-	4	-ion, -tion, -ation,-tion	4
7	in-, im- (in)	3	-able, -ible	2
8	over-	3	-al, -ial	1
9	mis-	3	-y	1
10	sub-	3	-ness	1
11	pre-	3	-ity, -ty	1
12	inter-	3	-ment	1
13	fore-	3	-ic	1
14	de-	2	-ous, -eous, -ious	1
15	trans-	2	-en	1
16	super-	1	-er (comparative)	1
17	semi-	1	-ive, -ative, -tive	1
18	anti-	1	-ful	1
19	mid-	1	-less	1
20	under- – (too little)	1	-est	1
	All Others	3	All Others	1

remembering that –tion indicates the word is a noun and that –ed usually forms the past tense of verbs can make it easier for readers to figure out words using these suffixes. Once students have grasped the concepts of prefixes, suffixes, and roots, you can easily teach them specific word parts. Only 20 prefixes make up 97 percent of the prefixed words in printed school English. Sixty-five percent of suffixed words end in –s, -es, -ed, or –ing. The preceding table shows a list of the most commonly used prefixes and suffixes in printed school English (Adams, 2007). Teaching your students just a few of these affixes can dramatically improve their vocabulary development. (Vacca et al, 2003, p. 308) found that third graders who were taught the first nine prefixes and suffixes in the chart and how to break down words into roots and suffixes outperformed a control group tested in measures of word meaning. Many lists containing hundreds of Greek and Latin roots are available, but teaching the meanings of roots may not be as useful to your students as teaching the affixes. (Steinmetz, 1999) have pointed out that the current meanings of many words do not resemble their historical roots. Trying to apply the ancient meanings of roots to figure out the meanings of words used today may only confuse students. However, telling students about the roots of words they are learning can help make those words more memorable by adding a story to what they know. For example, the following account of the origin of miniature reinforces the word's meaning.

The word **miniature** comes from the Latin *miniare,* which means

> "to color in." Before printing was invented, books were written a page at a time with pens and ink. Pictures in them, usually quite small, were painted by hand. The word *miniature* came to mean anything very small, especially a small portrait or a small copy or model of a larger object.

In content areas such as science, it may be useful to have students memorize roots that recur. Using word webs like the following can reinforce the relations among words incorporating these roots:

Word Part Web

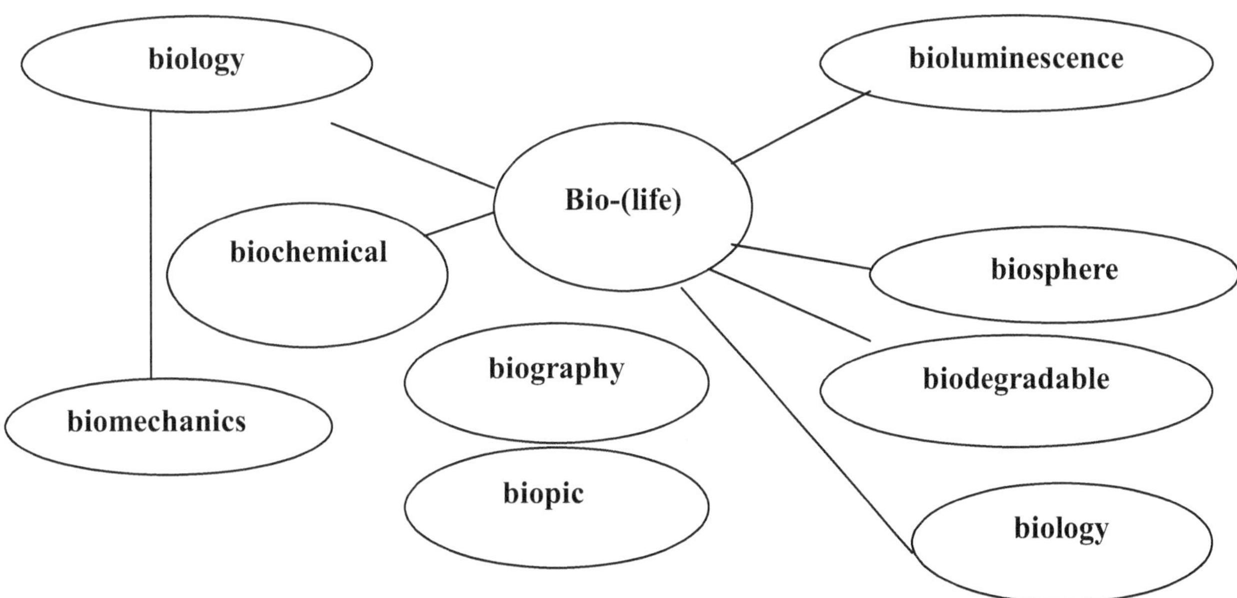

The strategy of using word parts is probably most effective when combined with other ways of acquiring words, such as context clues. Knowing how to break down words into parts will make them easier to tackle; learning prefixes, suffixes, and some roots will give students more tools for vocabulary growth.

USING GRAPHIC ORGANIZERS

Encouraging wide reading, using context, and employing word parts are excellent long term strategies for vocabulary development. The following are some additional activities that can deepen your students' word knowledge and expand your direct instruction of vocabulary.

CONCEPT OF DEFINITION MAPS

Concept of definition maps such as the following are graphic organizers that show the elements of a typical dictionary definition, including:

*The category to which the word belongs, labeled, "What is this?"

CONCEPT OF DEFINITION MAP

What is this?
A flesh eating animal

Examples

Examples
dog, bear, cat

Non- examples
Cow, sheep

Carnivore

What is it like?
Have sharp teeth or fangs. Consumes other animals. May eat foods other than meat

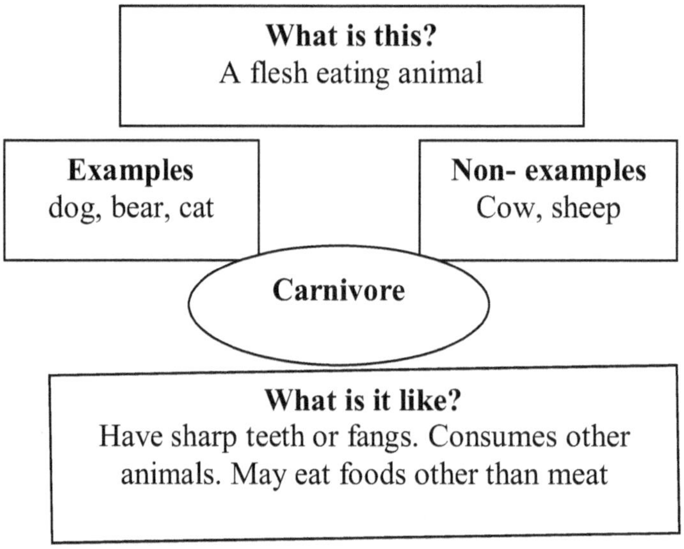

- Characteristics of the word, labeled. "What is it like?"
- Examples and non-examples of the word.

Students fill in the maps by referring to context, using their prior knowledge, and consulting dictionaries. The following map elucidates the meaning of *carnivore.*

After having the class completes the map, you may want to model how to write a definition using the information in the map. For example, you could say: "A carnivore is a mammal that eats flesh. A carnivore has fangs and consumes other animals. It may sometimes eat food that is not meat. Dogs, cats, and bears are some types of carnivores. "You can also have students write their own definition and then confirm them by looking the word up in the dictionary. They may revise their definitions after looking them up.

Semantic Maps

Semantic maps can be used to develop students understanding of a particular concept or group of thematically related words. For example, in teaching about dinosaurs, you might target the following vocabulary words: *ancestor, carnivore, gigantic, extinct,* and *ferocious.* Then begin instruction by having students brainstorm words related to the concept of dinosaurs. As they brainstorm, list their words on the board, making sure to include the targeted words. Discussion is key to semantic mapping. During the brainstorming session, have students discuss and define all of the words on the list. Help students refine their understanding of the words by asking them to group related words together to create a semantic map such as this one.

Semantic Map

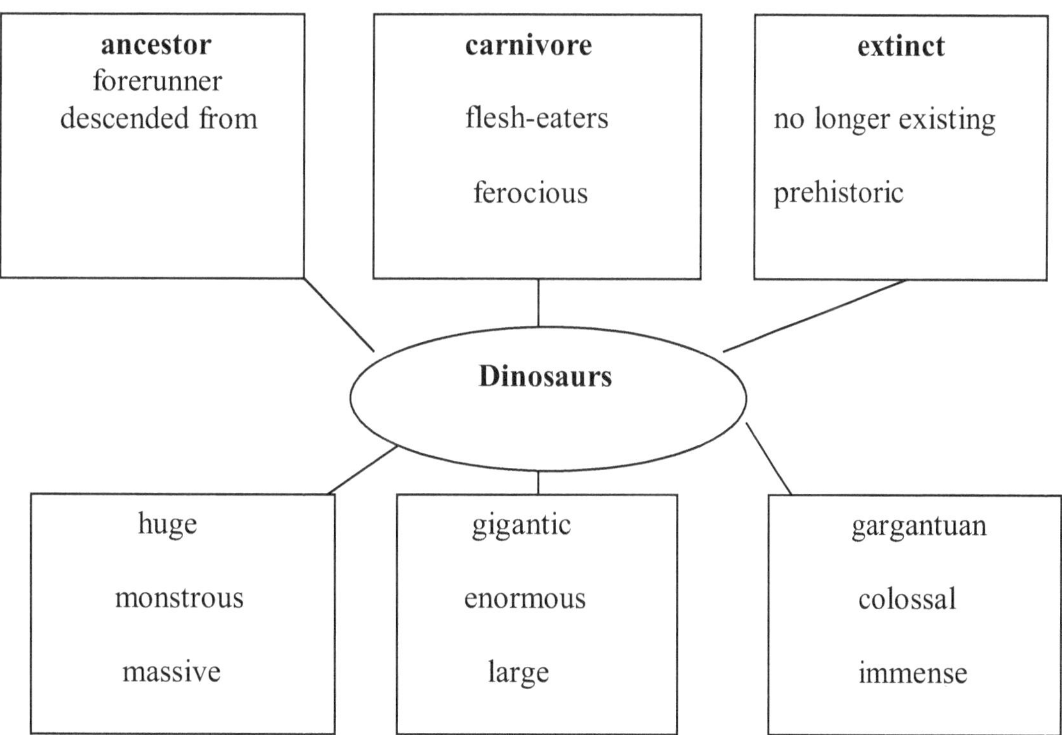

The target words are highlighted, and sections are left blank so that the class can fill in other categories after reading the selection, Semantic mapping is a good technique to use in content – area teaching, in which vocabulary words are thematically related. The technique works best as a group activity, since discussion helps students with smaller vocabularies learn all the words that are talked about. Advance learners will benefit from the extra exposure to words they have already learned

Semantic Feature Analysis

Another good technique to use in teaching words that share content is semantic feature analysis, which makes use of a grid, such as the following. The left-hand column contains the names of members of the category. For a unit on living creatures, you might write words such as: *dog, cat, hamster, tiger, buffalo, sparrow,* and *horse.* The top row of the grid lists features of the category's members such as: has *fur, has feathers, can fly, can be a pet, and runs on four legs.* Students should be encouraged to add terms to either the column or the row during discussion.

Semantic Feature Analysis

	Has fur	Has feathers	Can fly	Can be a pet	Runs on four legs
dog	+	-	-	+	+
cat	+	-	-	+	+
hamster	+	-	-	+	+
buffalo	?	-	-	-	+
tiger	+	-	-	-	+
sparrow	-	+	+	-	-
horse	?	-	-	?	+

After seeing the grid, groups of students or the whole class discusses whether the items in the columns are an example of the features across the top, marking (+) for positive examples, (-) for negative examples, and (?) for words that might be examples. As with semantic maps, discussion is key to clarifying the meanings of words in this activity. It is also an excellent technique to use in content areas such as social studies and science.

Comparing And Contrasting Venn Diagrams

Venn diagrams are another good graphic organizer to use, especially when teaching students to compare and contrast related concepts such as *apple* and *bananas, map* and *calendar, poetry* and *prose.*

The following diagram helps to clarify the similarities and differences between two related ideas.

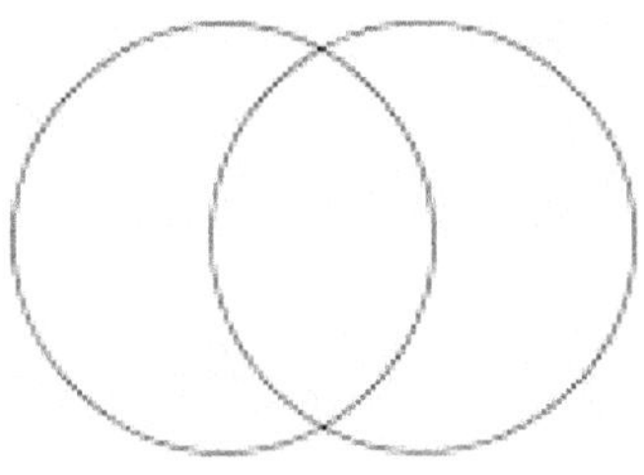

Using graphic organizers will provide your students with more exposures to words they are acquiring and will help them solidify the knowledge they've gained.

Extending Instruction Through Reading Aloud And Discussion

Although researchers have shown that it is the volume of reading rather than oral language that is the prime contributor to differences in students' vocabularies past the fourth grade, reading aloud to your students can also help them acquire words. Reading literature to students exposes them to rich language that they usually do not hear by everyday speech. Researchers have found that sixth graders learned about as many words from a single listening as they would from a single reading. Reading aloud can be a good strategy to use with students who have smaller vocabularies, although even advanced and older students will enjoy the activity. Additionally, discussion can greatly enhance any vocabulary instruction. Students with small vocabularies benefit from the knowledge contributed by their classmates, and misunderstandings of words can be elucidated publicly. Therefore, as students wait to be called on, they often practice responses silently. As a result, discussion reinforces vocabulary development. Discussions can be made more fun by having students act out or pantomime words or engage in debates about word meanings.

Since vocabulary growth is such a long process, drawing on a variety of approaches helps to prevent boredom. Some words require much more detailed instruction than others, certain activities such as semantic maps work best with words that are related in meaning. As you experienced with the strategies and techniques just described, you will be able to determine which ones will best help your students.

Graphic Organizers

Graphic organizers (some of which are also called concept maps, entity relationship charts, and mind maps) are a pictorial way of constructing knowledge and organizing information. They help the student convert and compress a lot of seemingly disjointed information into a structured, simple-to-read, graphic display. The resulting visual display conveys complex information in a simple-to-understand manner.

Increasing Understanding By Creating Graphic Organizers

The process of converting a mass of data/information/ideas into a graphic map gives the student an increased understanding and insight into the topic at hand. To create the map, the student must concentrate on the relationships between the items and examine the meanings attached to each of them. While creating a map, the student must also prioritize the information, determining which parts of the material are the most important and should be focused upon, and where each item should be placed in the map. The creation of graphic organizers also helps the student generate ideas as they develop and note their thoughts visually. The possibilities associated with a topic become clearer as the student's ideas are classified visually.

Uses of Graphic Organizers:

Graphic organizers can be used to structure writing projects, to help in problem solving, decision making, studying, planning research and brainstorming. adding color-coding and/or pictures to a graphic organizer further increases the utility and readability of the visual display.

The task at hand determines the type of graphic organizer that is appropriate. The following is a list of common graphic organizers - choose the format that best fits your topic.

Star: If the topic involves investigating attributes associated with a single topic, use a star diagram as your graphic organizer. Example: Finding methods that help your study skills (like taking notes, reading, doing homework, memorizing, etc.).

Spider: If the topic involves investigating attributes associated with a single topic, and then obtaining more details on each of these ideas, use a spider diagram as your graphic organizer. This is like the star graphic organizer with one more level of detail. Example: Finding methods that help your study skills (like taking notes, reading, memorizing, etc.), and investigating the factors involved in performing each of the methods.

Fishbone: If the topic involves investigating multiple cause-and-effect factors associated with a complex topic and how they inter-relate; use a fishbone diagram as your graphic organizer. Example: Examining the effects of improved farming methods.

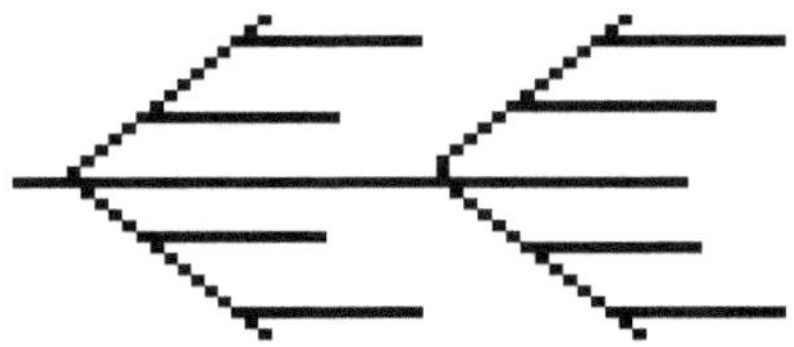

Cloud/Cluster: If the topic involves generating a web of ideas based on a stimulus topic, use a clustering diagram as your graphic organizer. Example: brainstorming.

Tree: If the topic involves a chain of events with a beginning and with multiple outcomes at each node (like a family tree), use a tree as your graphic organizer. Example: Displaying the probabilistic results of tossing coins.

Chain of Events: If the topic involves a linear chain of events, with a definite beginning, middle, and end, use a chain of events graphic organizer. Example: Analyzing the plot of a story.

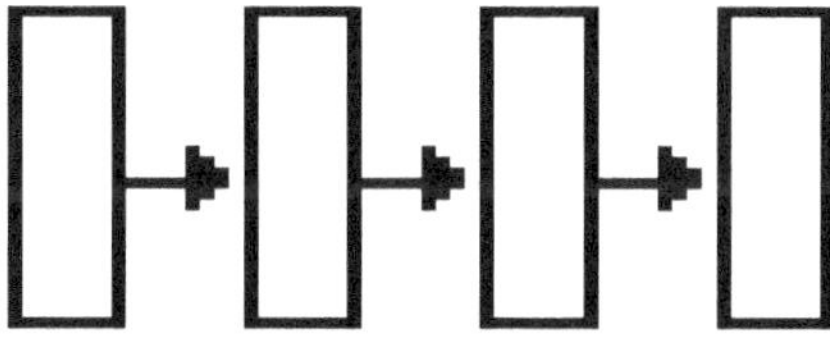

Continuum/Timeline: If the topic has definite beginning and ending points and a number of divisions or sequences in between, use a continuum/timeline. Example: Displaying milestones in a person's life.

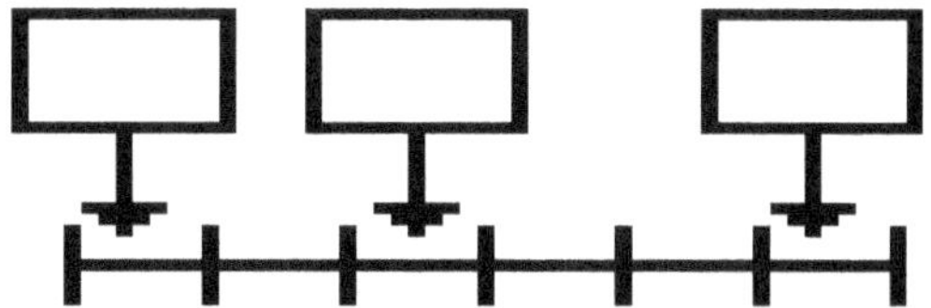

Clock: If the topic involves a clock-like cycle, use a clock graphic organizer. Example topic: Recording the events in a typical school day or making a story clock to summarize a story.

Cycle of Events: If the topic involves a recurring cycle of events, with no beginning and no end, use a cyclic graphic organizer. Example topic: Documenting the stages in the lifecycle of an animal.

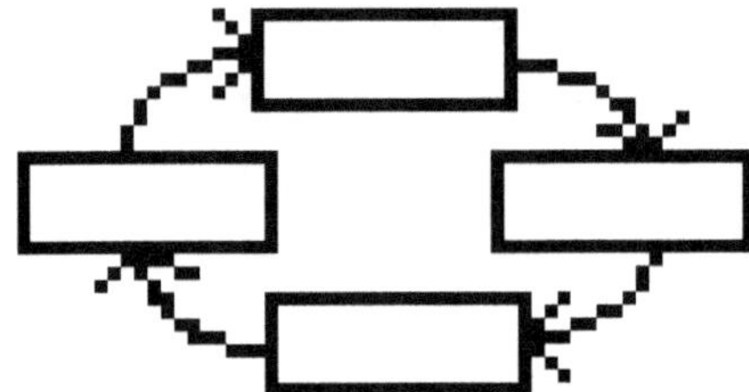

Flowchart: If the topic involves a chain of instructions to follow, with a beginning and multiple possible outcomes at some node, with rules at some nodes, use a flowchart. Example: Computer programmers sometimes use flowcharts to organize the algorithm before writing a program.

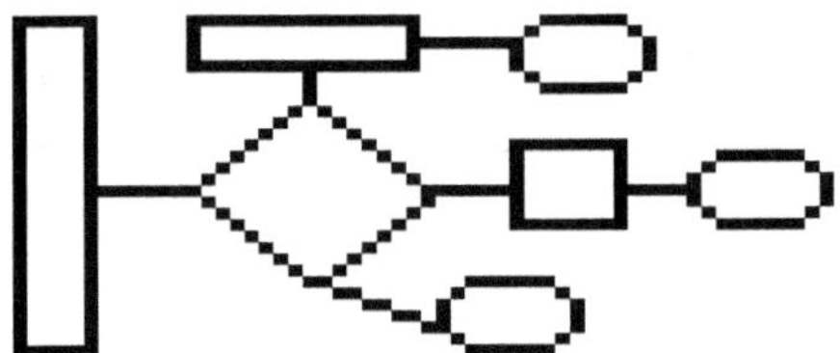

Venn Diagram: If the task involves examining the similarities and differences between two or three items, use a Venn diagram. Example: Examining the similarities and differences between fish and whales, or comparing a book and the accompanying movie.

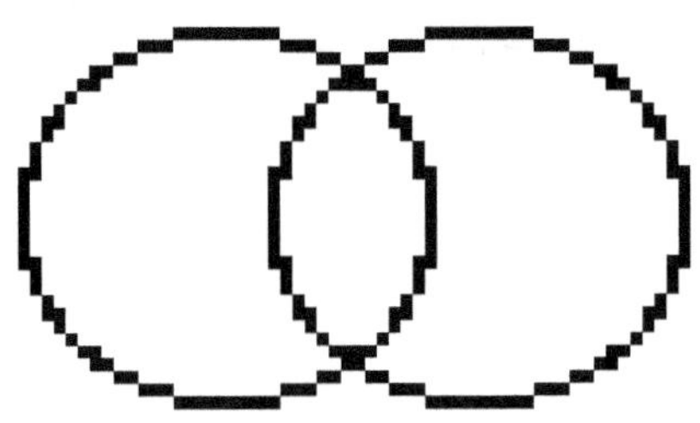

Chart/Matrix Diagram: If the task involves condensing and organizing data about traits of many items, use a chart/matrix. Example: Creating a display of key inventions, who invented them, when, where and why they were invented, etc.

Y-Chart Diagram: If the task involves analyzing and organizing with respect to three qualities, use a Y-Chart. Example: Fill out a Y-Chart to describe what you know about an animal, including what it looks like, what it sounds like, and what it feels like. Or describe a character in a book, including what the character looks like, sounds like, and how the character feels.

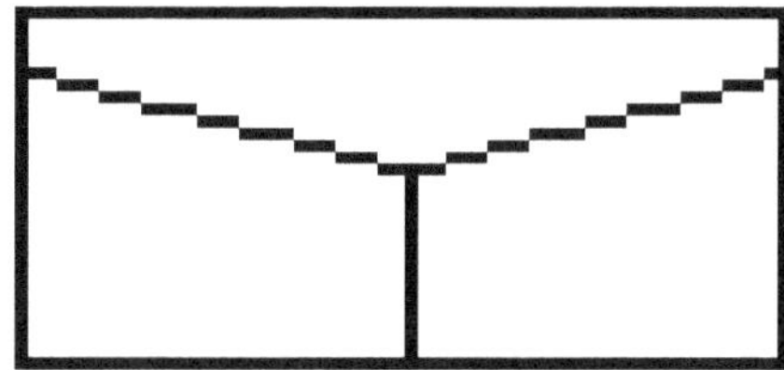

T-Chart Diagram: If the task involves analyzing or comparing with two aspects of the topic, use a T-Chart. Example: Fill out a T-Chart to evaluate the pros and cons associated with a decision.

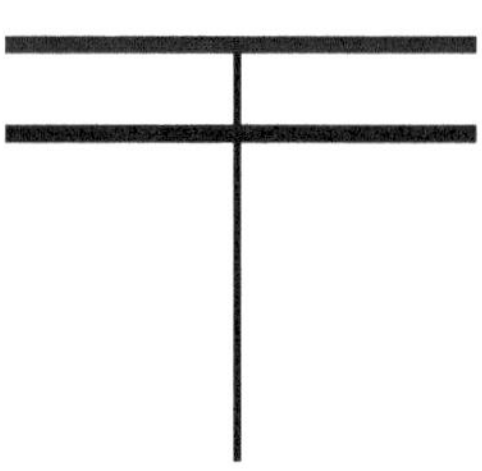

Fact/Opinion: If the task involves distinguishing the facts vs. the opinions in a theme or text, use fact/opinion charts. Example: Fill out a fact/opinion chart to evaluate the facts and opinions presented in a news article.

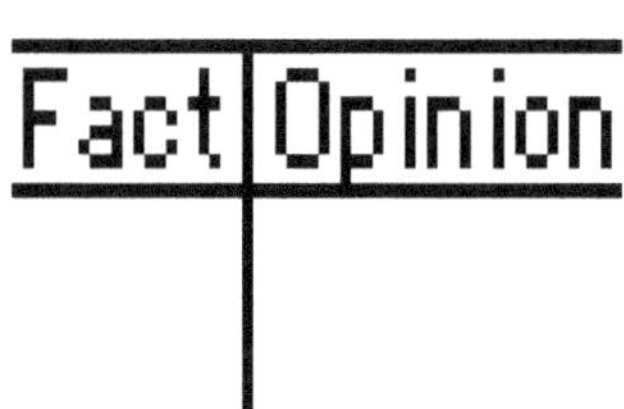

If the task involves analyzing the plusses, minuses, and implications of a decision or an action, use a PMI Chart. Example: Fill out a PMI Chart to help evaluate the positive, negative and interesting points associated with taking a new job.

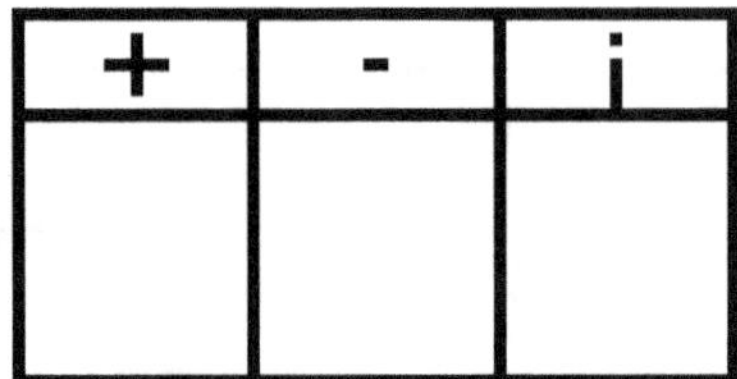

Decision Making Diagrams: If the task is making a decision, use a graphic organizer to enumerate possible alternatives and the pros and cons of each. Example: Fill out a decision making diagram to help decide which elective courses you'd like to take next quarter.

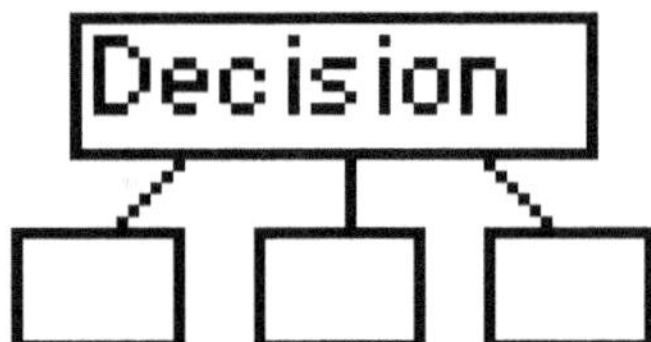

Semantic Feature Analysis Charts: If the task is comparing characteristics among a group of items, use Semantic Feature Analysis. Example: Fill out a Semantic Feature Analysis chart to compare and contrast the care needed for various pets.

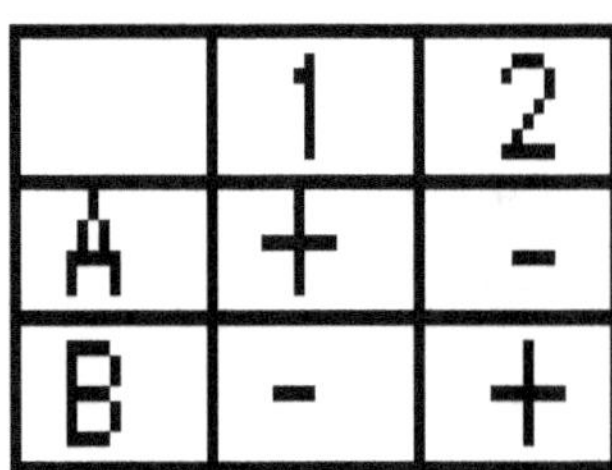

Cause and Effect Diagrams: If the task is examining possible causes and effects in a process, use a cause and effect graphic organizer. Example: Fill out a cause-and-effect diagram to trace the steps in a feedback loop.

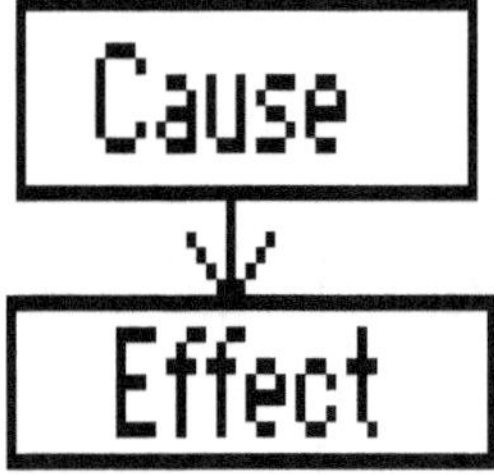

KWHL Diagram: If the task involves analyzing and organizing what you know and what you want to learn about a topic, use a KWHL chart. **K** stands for what you already KNOW about the subject. **W** stands for what you WANT to learn. **H** stands for figuring out HOW you can learn more about the topic. **L** stands for what you LEARN as you read. Example: Fill out a KWHL chart before, during, and after you read about a topic.

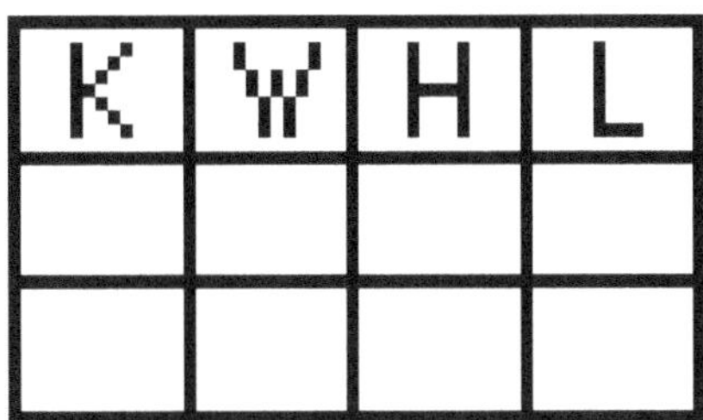

Pie Charts: If the task involves showing divisions with a group, use a pie chart. Example: Draw a pie chart to show what percentages of a population have blue eyes, green eyes, or brown eyes.

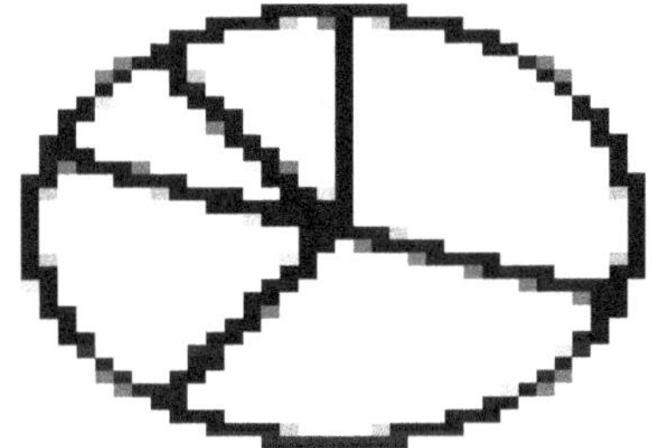

Vocabulary Map: Graphic organizers can be useful in helping a student learn new vocabulary words, having them list the word, its part of speech (noun, verb, adjective, adverb, etc.), a synonym, an antonym, a drawing that represents the word, and a sentence using the word.

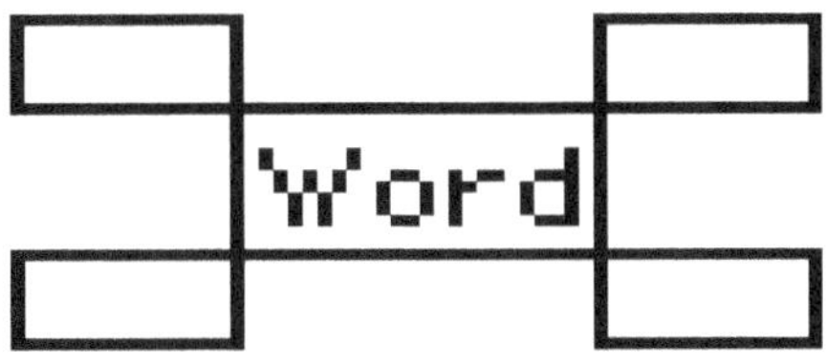

Paragraph Structure: These graphic organizers help you organize the structure of a paragraph, including a topic sentence, sentences with support details, and a conclusion sentence.

5 W's Diagram: If the task involves analyzing the Five W's (**W**ho, **W**hen, **W**here, **W**hat, and **W**hy) of a story or event. Example: Fill out a 5 W's Chart to help evaluate and understand the major points of a newspaper story.

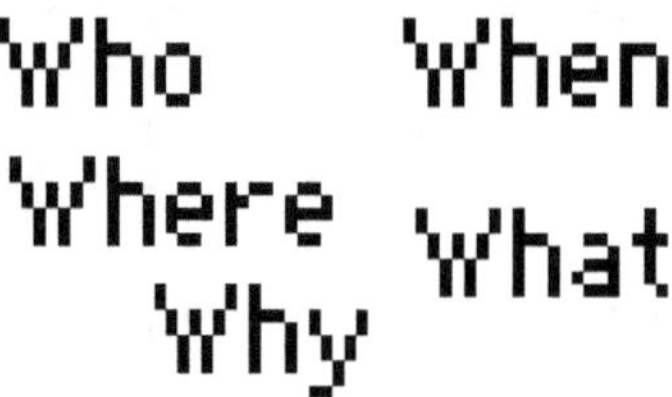

Story Map: Story maps can help a student summarize, analyze and understand a story or event.

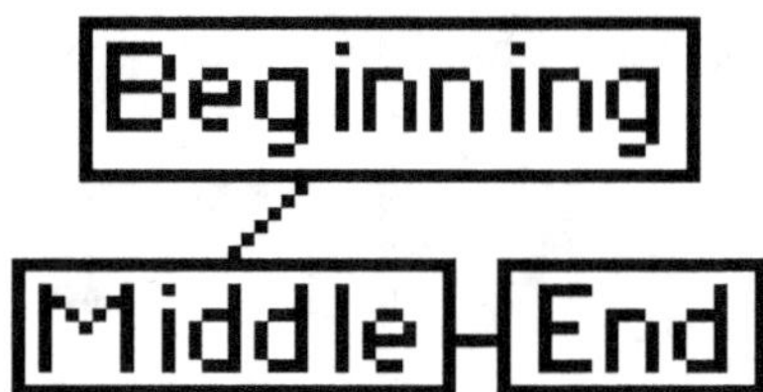

Character Traits: Graphic organizers help the student identify the traits of fictional characters by looking at events surrounding the character in the text.

Biography Diagrams Graphic organizers are useful to help prepare for writing a biography. Before writing, the graphic organizer prompts the student to think about and list the major events in the person's life.

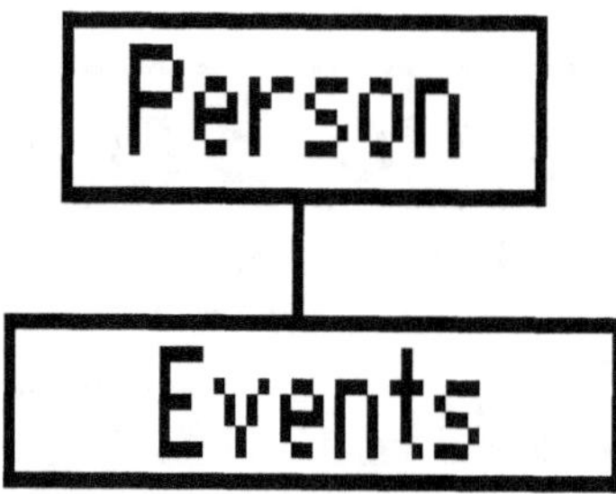

Animal Report Diagrams: Many graphic organizers are useful to help prepare for writing a report on animals. Before writing, the student should think about and list the major topics that will be researched and covered in the report.

Geography Report Diagrams: These graphic organizers are useful for doing a short report on a country or other area. The student draws a map and flag, and looks up basic information on the area.

Math Diagrams: Many graphic organizers are useful to learn and do math, include Venn diagrams, star diagrams, charts, flowcharts, trees, etc.

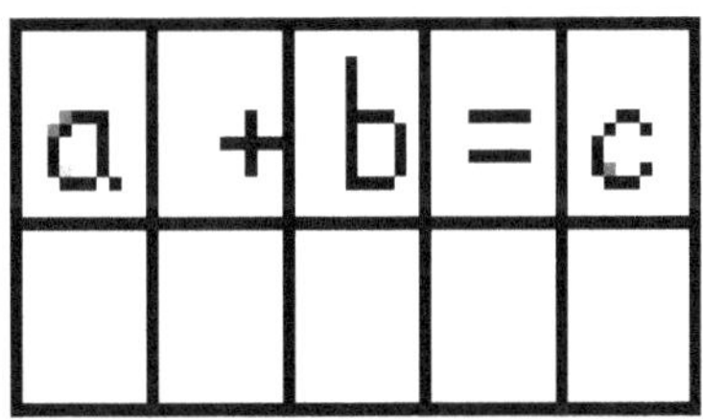

Scientific Method Diagrams: Graphic organizers used to prepare and organize a scientific experiment. **Diagrams** are a type of graphic organizer that condense and organize data about multiple traits, fact, or attributes associated with a single topic. Diagrams are useful for basic brainstorming about a topic or simply listing all the major traits related to a theme.

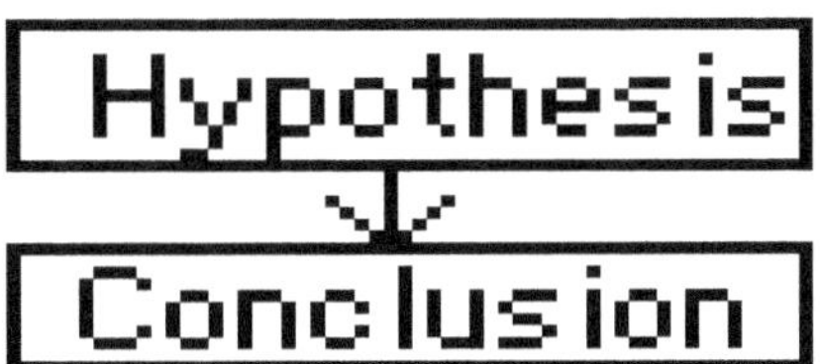

For example, a scroll diagram can be used to create a graphic display describing all you know about dinosaurs (when they lived, what kinds there were, how big they were, what they ate, where fossils have been found, etc.) or a graphic display of methods that help your skills (like taking notes, reading, doing homework, memorizing, etc.). Another use is a diagram used to describe the key points of a story or event, noting the 5 W's: who, when, where, what, and why

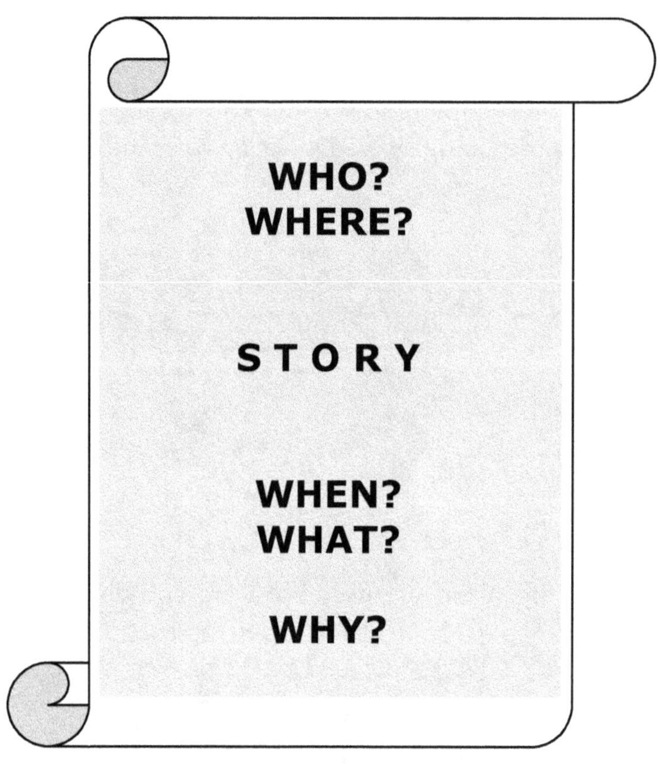

CHAPTER VII

COMPREHENSION

Reading comprehension can be defined as the level of understanding of a passage or text. For normal reading rates (around 200-220 words per minute) an acceptable level of comprehension is above 75%.Reading comprehension can be improved by: Training the ability to self assess comprehension, actively test comprehension using questionnaires, and by improving metacognition (LeFevre & Richardson, 2001) Teaching conceptual and linguistic knowledge is also advantageous. Self assessment can be conducted by summarizing, and elaborative interrogation, and those skills will gradually become more automatic through practice. In some situations, reading comprehension is often tested, but is seldom taught (Ekwall, 1992). Years ago, reading instruction focused on teaching decoding skills, while comprehension consisted of simple questions and retelling (Carnine, 2006). It is crucial that young students are taught the importance of getting meaning from reading (Ekwall, 1992). It is essential that they understand that the reading process is more than just decoding words. Prior to the 1970s, the process of reading comprehension was viewed as the reader's ability to restate the text (Brooks, 2004).

Historical strategies include worksheets, which did not engage students, resulting in not much being gained by these activities (Brownell, 2004). Today it is known that skillful readers use prior knowledge, make connections, visualize, infer, ask questions, determine importance, and synthesize the materials that they read (Grimes, 2004). As the amount of background knowledge concerning a text increases, the ability to comprehend the text correlates (Pardo, 2004). When skillful readers use their schema, their known information is integrated with their new information through a series of connections (Pardo, 2004). Skillful readers verify that what they are reading makes sense and if not use strategies to comprehend the text when it stops making sense (Pardo, 2004). Struggling readers need to be taught to fix their reading when it does not make sense. Teachers need to provide explicit instruction in using reading strategies. It is imperative that teachers "show not tell" how skillful readers read.

CAUSES OF READING COMPREHENSION DIFFICULTIES

There are multiple risk factors involved when teaching struggling and At-Risk readers. These factors include: attendance problems, behavior problems, low academic achievement, low socioeconomic status, mobility issues, retention, and Attention Deficit Disorder or Attention Deficit Hyperactivity Disorder

(Brooks, 2004) Struggling readers may come from underprivileged literacy environments, leading to fewer oral language and emergent literacy skills, and limited prior knowledge (Brownell, 2004; and Brooks, 2004). Some parents of the targeted group in the study rarely take time to read to their children, or may not have the ability to do so according to students. This challenges the ability of teachers to successfully educate students (Brooks, 2004). Struggling and at-risk readers may have fewer schemas to help them comprehend while reading. Teachers need to increase schema in the classroom as much as possible. Learning dispositions can be the greatest obstacle to learning, possibly sabotaging the learning possibilities of reading experiences (Kidd, 2004). Struggling readers differ from skilled readers in their use of world knowledge while comprehending texts, as well as monitoring comprehension and fix-up strategies. For some, they lack the knowledge needed in order to rectify their breakdown in comprehension (Massey, 2003). They may fail to understand keywords, and the way that sentences relate to one another. Comprehension problems may also be due to difficulties in reading fluently (Parker, 2004).Fluency is vital for students to develop effective reading comprehension skills. Readers lacking fluency spend excessive time decoding, leading to less short-term memory available for comprehension.

Engagement and Motivation To Read

Motivation to read can impact a reader's persistence in reading. Students with higher amounts of motivation are more likely to apply the use of comprehension strategies while reading (Pardo, 2004). Although there are many motivational factors that are not within the teachers' control, teachers are able to motivate students to read by providing interesting texts, allowing choices to be made as levels of engagement increase, so does comprehension (Grimes, 2003)..

Activation Of Prior Knowledge

Activation of prior knowledge makes up a great amount of the process of reading comprehension. Teachers should attempt to activate as much prior knowledge as possible prior to reading the text, allowing students to apply the prior knowledge use while reading (Pardo, 2004). They also need to teach how to decipher useful background knowledge from other background knowledge. Strategies to effectively activate prior knowledge include: brain storming, predicting, pre-reading questioning, and topic talking (Brooks, 2004). Picture walks before read-alouds, guided and independent reading are also effective... Reading aloud, thinking aloud, along with teacher modeling activating schema, and making connections enables readers to apply this information while they read (Pardo, 2004).

For children in K-12 public schools in the United States, building reading comprehension skills to pass the high-stake tests mandated by the No Child Left Behind Laws is a top priority. Many parents when informed that their children need to build comprehension skills do not know where to start. Effective reading comprehension is the culmination of mastering vocabulary, phonics, fluency, and reading comprehension skills. The reading skills pyramid illustrates how these skills are expected to be built in most public schools (Dickenson & Tabors, 2001)

Reading comprehension skills separates the "passive" unskilled reader from the "active" readers. Skilled readers don't just read, they interact with the text. To help a beginning reader understand this concept, you might make them privy to the dialogue readers have with themselves while reading (Harris and Sipay (1990)

Skilled readers, for instance:

- Predict what will happen next in a story using clues presented in text
- Create questions about the main idea, message, or plot of the text
- Monitor understanding of the sequence, context, or characters
- Clarify parts of the text which have confused them
- Connect the events in the text to prior knowledge or experience

Reading Comprehension Testing

Comprehension testing is very useful in improving reading comprehension, not only because it gives the teacher a measure of progress, but it supplements the reader's perception of his or her own ability. Learning readers commonly fail to accurately assess their own comprehension. A comprehension test can accelerate their ability to self-assess their own comprehension levels as they progress. However, a poorly constructed reading comprehension test can deceive the learner and disturb progress. Indeed, it has been found that poorly constructed tests often train the reader to miss-assess their own reading performance. Reading comprehension is best tested using carefully constructed questions which quiz natural or non-concocted passages of text. The questions themselves can be requests to summarize, open ended questions; Cloze formats, and carefully constructed multiple choice questions (Hiebert, 1999)

The multiple choice format must use questions that quiz the overall meanings of the text, the details and the most important meaning of the words. The background of the reader must be taken into account. For example, if an answer is general knowledge, then it will not measure the comprehension of the passage, but the memory of that knowledge. Likewise, the questions should not give clues to the answers of other questions. In this way it makes the multiple choice format hard to devise. Some Speed reading courses and books design their comprehension tests using the antithesis of these factors in order to mislead the reader into believing that their reading comprehension has improved with increased speed. However, a valid pre and post test can be used to effectively measure improvement. The purpose of reading is comprehension. How do we teach children to comprehend more difficult and varied texts? Until recently, we had few answers. But research from recent decades has provided a general outline of how to effectively teach reading comprehension.

1. **Effective comprehension instruction requires purposeful and explicit teaching.** Effective teachers of reading are clear about their purposes. They know what they are trying to help a child achieve and how to accomplish their goal. They provide scaffolded instruction in research-tested strategies (predicting, thinking aloud, attending to text structure, constructing visual representations, generating questions and summarizing). Scaffolded instruction includes explicit explanation and modeling of a strategy, discussion of why and when it is useful, and coaching in how to apply it to novel texts (National Reading Panel (2000)

2. **Effective reading instruction requires classroom interactions that support the understanding of specific texts.**
   Effective teachers have a repertoire of techniques for enhancing children's comprehension of specific texts, including discussion, writing in response to reading, and multiple encounters with complex texts. They are clear about the purposes of teacher- and student-led discussions of texts, and include a balance of lower and higher-level questions focusing on efferent and aesthetic response. Well-designed writing assignments deepen children's learning from text (Dickinson, & Tabors, (2001).

4. **Effective reading comprehension instruction starts before children read conventionally.**
   Children in preschool and kindergarten develop their comprehension skills through experiences that promote oral and written language skills, such as discussions, play activities, retellings, and emergent readings. Early childhood environments can be made literacy-rich through thoughtful inclusion of appropriate materials and practices. Reading and rereading a wide variety of texts contributes to both phonemic awareness and comprehension (Duke, N. (2000).

5. **Effective reading comprehension teaches children the skills and strategies used by expert readers.**
   Expert readers are active readers who use text and their own knowledge to build a model of meaning, and then constantly revise that model as new information becomes available. They consider the author's intentions and style when judging a text's validity, and determine the purposes that the text can serve in their lives—how it can further their knowledge, deepen their enjoyment,

and expand their ways of examining and communicating with the world (They also vary their reading strategy according to their purpose and the characteristics of the genre, deciding (LeFevre & Richardson, (2001). whether to read carefully or impressionistically.

6. **Effective reading comprehension instruction requires careful analysis of text to determine its appropriateness for particular students and strategies.**

Teachers analyze each text to determine its potential challenges and match it with their goals. They consider conceptual and decoding demands and apply strategies to meet those challenges. Interactions with texts requiring minimal teacher support help hold children accountable as independent readers. Scaffolded experiences ensure that all children are exposed to high-level text and interactions.

7. **Effective reading comprehension instruction builds on and results in knowledge, vocabulary, and advanced language development.**

Children are better able to comprehend texts when they are taught to make connections between what they know and what they are reading. Good comprehension instruction helps them make these connections more effectively. Vocabulary knowledge is an important part of reading comprehension, and good vocabulary instruction involves children actively in learning word meanings, as well as relating words to contexts and other known words. Teaching about words (including morphology) improves children's comprehension (Paris & Winograd, (2001).

8. **Effective reading comprehension instruction pervades all genres and school subjects.**

Children need to read in a wide variety of genres—not only narrative, but informational, procedural, biographical, persuasive, and poetic. They will only learn to do so through experience and instruction. Each school subject requires the ability to read in specific genres; therefore, comprehension should be taught in all subjects.

9. **Effective reading comprehension instruction actively engages children in text and motivates them to use strategies and skills.**

Effective teachers create an environment in which children are actively involved in the reading process. In such an environment children read more, which in turn improves their comprehension and knowledge. Children need to be motivated to learn and apply skills and strategies during reading.

10. **Good comprehension instruction requires assessments that inform instruction and monitor student progress.**

The use of multiple assessments provides specific and timely feedback to inform instruction and monitor student progress toward research-based benchmarks. Good assessment identifies students' comprehension levels as they develop from preschool to advanced grade levels, and helps the teacher to evaluate each child's need for support in areas such as language development, strategy, and the application of knowledge. Effective assessment also enables teachers to reliably interpret data and communicate results to students, parents, and colleague (Hiebert, 1999).

11. **Effective reading comprehension instruction requires continuous teacher learning** about the processes and techniques detailed in the previous nine principles and ways to use such knowledge to develop the comprehension skills and strategies of all students. Working closely with their peers in school-based or interest-based learning communities, effective teachers learn to use assessment data, reflections on their own practice, and moment-by-moment feedback from children to vary the support they provide to students with different levels of expertise and confident

Reading Comprehension instruction and Mental Modeling helps to accelerates improvement of reading comprehension. The definition and value of mental modeling is thinking aloud to demonstrate inner scripts such as a proficient reader/thinker might use to "strategize" complex cognitive operations and in ways that entice a learner to imitate and improvise such scripts for use in analogous situations. It also is known as "cognitive apprenticeship," a term that conveys the historical origins of mental modeling in teaching crafts, though now recognized for its robust value in conveying habits of mind. Mental modeling is efficient and effective because students tend to emulate (copy and personalize) broader characteristics of the model, such as social poise, language and demeanor, as well as more narrowly defined objectives of traditional teaching of Intuitive, But Elusive Concept of Mental modeling is the fundamental process of natural language acquisition. Parents incidentally use mental modeling because they intuitively realize that it imparts culture and values by becoming part of inner-speech which mediates and self-regulates attitudes and behavior. Nonetheless, its use in formal education had been delayed until recent times due to pragmatic and theoretical problems. At a practical level, the challenges were in how to get and hold student attention, and in reducing the social consequences of early and awkward learning in the social setting of the classroom. At a theory level, there was the issue of whether invisible mental processes could be adequately displayed for emulation and refinement as thinking/learning strategies. Lev Vygotsky wrote with considerable insight into the interactions of the two competing constructs of the time, behaviorism and social-imitation learning theory. Importantly, neither theory held a sound explanation for two other intuitively evident aspects of cognitive growth; vicarious and self-regulated learning. Vygotsky, and others, such as Jerome Bruner, wrote plaintively for discovery and social collaboration and more holistic, top-down teaching, - or, what today would be called constructivism. However, neither was able to define teaching methods that concretely captured these qualities.

Proof-of-Principle

A proof-of-principle emerged in the form of a method for improving reading comprehension based on mental modeling. This was notable since there was an unspoken belief that comprehension and intellectual capacity, which had been found to be highly correlated, were nearly one and therefore that each was relatively immutable. Using a customized form of mental modeling, the Reciprocal Questioning (Request) Procedure was shown to significantly improve reading comprehension with remedial level readers (Manzo, 1968; 1969). Request is a relatively simple procedure that has the teacher and students take turns asking questions about the first few sentences of a reading selection. The teacher models this comprehension, problem-solving strategy in the form of questions for independently setting a purpose for reading, and in think aloud reflections in answer to student questions. Students quickly began to imitate both the teacher's questions and question "answering" strategies; they imitated and emulated the mental operations of models. Mental modeling appeared efficient, non-sequential, and holistic, but it also seemed to require certain supportive conditions...

Conditions for Effective Mental Modeling

Mental modeling seems to require an opposable thumb. Reciprocity appears to play this role. It permits teacher and students to pick-up on one another's "language of thinking" in an admittedly unnatural, but robust instructional, conversation. The procedure requires "rotation" away from the teacher's natural tendency to control talk, and inadvertent, repressive power over student talk. It also creates a diagnostic dialogue from which the teacher can further identify particular student needs and coach students in specifically prescribed strategic scripts: Reciprocal mental modeling reveals but does not publicly expose student needs. It also offers students scaffold opportunities to try-out thinking strategies in a low-risk environment in which they can vicariously learn by observing others until they are ready to venture out into the instructional conversation. There is a foreboding: reciprocal modeling that can mirror back a teacher's quirks of language and thought as well as proficiencies (Perfetti (1995). However, the reciprocal dialogue informs and shapes teacher question asking and answering as well as that of students.

Mental Modeling Is Broadly Applicable

Reciprocal Mental Modeling is a paradigm that can be applied in a variety of cognitive enrichment formats such as in teaching phonics and in language development through reciprocal inquiry over pictures. These uses are less well known, and probably in need of further specification.

REFERENCES

Abbott, M. (2000). Identifying reliable generalizations for spelling words: The importance of multilevel analysis. The Elementary School Journal 101(2), 233-245.

Adams, Marilyn Jager (1990). *Beginning to Read: Thinking and Learning About Print.*Mass Cambridge, MIT Press. ISBN 0-262-51076-6

Aiex, Nola Kortner (1990). "Debate and Communication Skills." ERIC Digest. Bloomington, IN: ERIC Clearinghouse on Reading, English, and Communication. [ED 321 334]

Aldridge, J. (2003). Rethinking the No Child Left Behind Act of 2001. Childhood Education, 80, 45-47.

Baker, Scott K., et al (1995). "Vocabulary Acquisition: Curricular and Instructional Implications for Diverse Learners." Technical Report No. 14. Eugene, OR: National Center to Improve the Tools of Educators. [ED 386 861]

Barton, J., and R. Calfee (1989). "Theory Becomes Practice: One Program." in Diane Lapp et al (Eds.), Content Area Reading and Learning: Instructional Strategies. Englewood Cliffs, NJ: Prentice Hall. [ED 304 673]

Bear, Donald R., et al (1996). Words Their Way: Word Study for Phonics, Vocabulary, and Spelling Instruction. New York: Merrill. [ED 386 685

Beck, I., & McKeown, M. (2001). Text talk: Capturing the benefits of read-aloud experiences for young children. The Reading Teacher, 55(1), 10-20

Berninger, V.W., Abbott, R.D., Billingsley, F., & Nagy, W. (2001). Processes underlying timing and fluency of reading: Efficiency, automaticity, coordination, and morphological awareness. In M.Wolf (Ed.), *Time, Fluency, and Dyslexia.* Timonium, MD: York Press

Berry, Kathleen S. (1985). "Talking to Learn Subject Matter/Learning Subject Matter Talk." Language Arts, 62(1), 34-42. [EJ 309 762

Blachman, B. A., Ball, E. W., Black, R. & Tangel, D. M. (2000). Road to the Code. Baltimore, MD: Paul H. Brookes Publishing Co.

Black, R. & Tangel, D. M. (2000). Road to the Code. Baltimore, MD: Paul H. Brookes Publishing Co

Bowers, P. G. (1993). Text reading and rereading Predictors of fluency beyond word recognition. Journal of Reading Behavior, 25, 133-153

(Brabham, E. G., and S. K. Villaume. "Building Walls of Words." Reading Teacher 54 no. 7 (April 2001): 700-702.:

Brentari, Diane (1998). *A prosodic model of sign language phonology*. Cambridge, MA: MIT Press

Brooks, M., Brownell, M. T., Kidd, S., Carnine, D.W., Elkwall, E.E., Grimes, S., Massey, D., Pardo, L.S., Parker, R et al (2004). Teaching Reading Comprehension to Struggling and At-Risk Readers.

Bruce Harrell. Speech-language pathologist. Retrieved on 2007-03-28 Blachman, B. A., Ball, E. W.,

Calkins, L. (2001). *The art of teaching reading.* New York: Addison-Wesley Educational Publishers, Inc.

Cattell, M. (1886). The time it takes to see and name objects. *Mind*, 2, 63-85.

Christen William L., and Thomas J. Murphy (1991). "Increasing Comprehension by Activating Prior Knowledge." ERIC Digest. Bloomington, IN: ERIC Clearinghouse on Reading, English, and Communication. [ED 328 885]

Conrad, N., Gong, Y., Sipp, L., & Wright, L. (2004), USING TEXT TALK AS A GATEWAY TO CULTURALLY RESPONSIVE TEACHING. Early Childhood Education Journal, 31(3), 187-192

Cooter, Robert B., Jr. (1991). "Storytelling in the Language Arts Classroom." Reading Research and Instruction, 30(2), 71-76. [EJ 424 278]

de Lacy, Paul. (2007). The Cambridge Handbook of Phonology. Cambridge University Press. ISBN 0-521-84879-2

Dahl, P. (1974). An experimental program for teaching high speed word recognition and comprehension skills (Rep. No. Final report project #3-1154). Washington, DC: National Institute of Education

Denckla, M. B. & Rudel, R.G. (1976). Rapid automatized naming (R.A.N.): Dyslexia differentiated from other learning disabilities. Neuropsychological, 14: 471-479

Dickinson, D. K., & Tabors, P. O. (2001). Beginning literacy with language: Young children learning at home & school. Baltimore: Paul H. Brookes Publishing

Duke, N. (2000). 3.6 minutes per day: The scarcity of informational texts in first grade. Reading Research Quarterly, 35: 202—224

Gambell, Trevor J. (1988). "Linguistics and Literacy Teaching." Paper presented at the World Conference of Applied Linguistics (Sydney, Australia). [ED 299 816

Goldstein, P (2004), HELPING YOUNG CHILDREN WITH SPECIAL NEEDS DEVELOP VOCABULARY. Early Childhood Education Journal, 32(1), 39-43.

Harris, T. L., and R. E. Hodges. eds. The Literacy Dictionary. Newark, Del.: International Reading Association, 1995.

Harris and Sipay (1990) *How to Increase Reading Ability* New York: Oxford University Press

Hart, T., & Risely, B. (1995). Meaningful differences in the early experience of young American children. Baltimore: Brookes.

Hiebert, E. H. (1999). Text matters in learning to read. (CIERA Report 1-001). Ann Arbor: CIERA

Hodapp, Joan B., and Albert F. Hodapp (1996). "Vocabulary Packs and Cued Spelling: Intervention Strategies." Paper presented at the Annual Convention of the National Association of School Psychologists (Atlanta). [ED 396 271]

Holbrook, Hilary Taylor (1983). "ERIC/RCS Report: Oral Language: A Neglected Language Art?" Language Arts, 60(2), 255-58. [EJ 276 124

Honig, A. (2004), HOW BABIES USE GESTURES TO COMMUNICATE. Scholastic Early Childhood Today, 26-28

Indiana Department of Education. (2000). *Indiana's academic standards: English/language arts.* Indianapolis, IN: Author.

Kameenui, E. J., Simmons, D. C., Good, R. H., & Harn, B. A. (2001). The use of fluency-based measures in early identification and evaluation of intervention efficacy in schools. In M.Wolf (Ed.), *Time, Fluency, and Dyslexia*: New-York: York Press.

Kueker, Joan (1990). "Prereading Activities: A Key to Comprehension." Paper presented at the International Conference on Learning Disabilities (Austin, TX). [ED 360 785]

LaBerge, D., & Samuels, S. J. (1974). Toward a theory of automatic information processing in reading. Cognitive Psychology, 6, 293-323.

LeFevre, D., & Richardson, V. (2001). Staff development in early reading intervention programs: The facilitator (CIERA Report 3-011). Ann Arbor: CI

Lemke, J. L. (1989). "Making Text Talk." Theory-into-Practice, 28(2), 136-41. [EJ 415 815]

Listening and Speaking in the English Language Arts Curriculum K-12. 1989 Field Test Edition. Albany, NY: New York State Education Department. [ED 335 726]

Lyle, Susan (1993). "An Investigation into Ways in Which Children Talk Themselves into Meaning." Language and Education, 7(3), 181-87. [EJ 485 116]

Manzo, A.V. (1968). *Improving reading comprehension through reciprocal questioning* (Doctoral dissertation, Syracuse University, Syracuse, NY,

Manzo, A.V. (1969) ReQuest: a method for improving reading comprehension through reciprocal questioning. *Journal of Reading*, 13, 123-126.

Manzo, A. V., Manzo, (2002) U.C. in *Mental Modeling in Literacy in America: an encyclopedia of History, theory and practice* (Ed. B. Guzzetti) Santa Barbara: California, ABC CLIO publisher. I, p. 344.

Massey, S. (2004), TEACHER-CHILD CONVERSATION IN THE PRESCHOOL CLASSROOM. Massey, S. Early Childhood Education Journal, 31(4), 227-231

Mather N & Sam Goldstein (2001)

McKeown, Margaret G., and Isabel L. Beck (1988). "Learning Vocabulary: Different Ways for Different Goals," Remedial and Special Education (RASE), 9(1), 42-46. [EJ 367 432]

Meyer, M. S. & Felton, R. H. (1999). Repeated reading to enhance fluency: Old approaches and new directions. Annals of Dyslexia, 49, 283-306.

Moore, David W., et al (1989). Prereading Activities for Content Area Reading and Learning. Newark, DE: International Reading Association. [ED 300 786]

Nagy, William E., et al (1985). "Learning Word Meanings from Context: How Broadly Generalizable?" Technical Report No. 347. Urbana, IL: Center for the Study of Reading. [ED 264 546]

Nagy, William (1988). Teaching Vocabulary to Improve Reading Comprehension. Urbana, IL: National Council of Teachers of English; Newark, DE: International Reading Association. [ED 298 471]

National Reading Panel. (2007, May 30). In *Wikipedia,* Retrieved 21:44, Augusthttp://en.wikipedia

National Reading Panel (2000). Report of the national reading panel. Washington, DC: Government Printing Office

Nelson-Herber, Joan (1986). "Expanding and Refining Vocabulary in Content Areas." Journal of Reading, 29, 626-33.

Neuman, S. (1999). Creating continuity in early literacy: Linking home and school with a culturally responsive approach. In L. B. Gambrell, L. M. Morrow, S. B. Neuman, & M. Pressley (Eds.), Best practices in literacy instruction (pp. 258-270). New York: The Guilford Press.

Ontario Government (2003). Reading Readiness.

Paris, S. G., & Winograd, P. (2001). The role of self-regulated learning in contextual teaching: Principles and practices for teacher education (CIERA Archives 01-04). Ann Arbor: CIERA

Perfetti (1995) *Reading Ability* New York: Oxford University Press *Ability*. Longman

Reutzel, D. & Cooper, R. (2000). Teaching children to read: Putting the pieces together (3rd ed.). Saddle River, NJ: Prentice Hall, Inc

Rowell, E. (1998). A letter a week, a story a day, and some missed opportunities along the way: A study of literacy in pre-kindergarten classes. Child Study Journal, 28, 201-211.

Ruddiman, Joan, et al (1993). "Open to Suggestion." Journal of Reading, 36(5), 400-09. [EJ 459 161]

Ryan & Cooper (2004)

Samuels, S.J. (1985). Automaticity and repeated reading. In Reading education: Foundations for a literate America, eds. J. Osborn, P.T. Wilson, and R.C. Anderson. Lexington, MA: Lexington Books.

Schickedanz, J., (2004), A FRAMEWORK AND SUGGESTED GUIDELINES FOR PREKINDERGARTEN CONTENT STANDARDS. The Reading Teacher, 58(1), 95-97

Schwartz, Robert M., and Taffy Raphael (1985). "Concept of Definition: A Key to Improving Students' Vocabulary." Reading Teacher, 39(2), 198-205. [EJ 325 191]

Seefeldt, C. (2004) HELPING CHILDREN COMMUNICATE. Scholastic Early Childhood Today, 36, 39, 41

Snow, C. (2002). Ensuring reading success for African American children. In B. Bowman (Ed.), Love to read (pp. 17-30). Washington, DC: National Black Child Development Institute.

Stabb, Claire (1986). "What Happened to the Sixth Graders: Are Elementary Students Losing Their Need to Forecast and to Reason?" Reading Psychology, 7(4), 289-96. [EJ 348 985]

Storch, S., & Whitehurst, G. (2002). Oral language and code-related precursors to reading: Evidence from a longitudinal structural model. Developmental Psychology, 38, 934-947.Top of Form

Strickland, D. (2004), WORKING WITH FAMILIES AS PARTNERS IN EARLY LITERACY. The Reading Teacher, 58(1), 86-88.

Szymborski, Julie Ann (1995). Vocabulary Development: Context Clues versus Word Definitions. M.A. Project, Kean College of New Jersey. [ED 380 757]

Wilkinson, Molly (1994). "Using Student Stories to Build Vocabulary in Cooperative Learning Groups." Clearing House, 67(4), 221-23. [EJ 486 167]

Willmington, S. Clay (1993). "Oral Communication Skills Necessary for Successful Teaching." Educational Research Quarterly, 16(2), 5-10. [EJ 480 434]

Woodward, C., Haskins, G., Schaefer, G., & Smolen, L. Young Children, 2004, 59(4), 92-95.LET'S TALK: A Different Approach to Oral Language Development.

Wolf, M. (1986). Rapid Alternating Stimulus Naming in the Developmental Dyslexia's. Brain and Language, 27: 360-379.

Wolf, M. (Ed.) (2001). *Time, Fluency, and Dyslexia.* Timonium, MD: York Press.

Wolf, M., & Bowers, P. (1999). The "Double-Deficit Hypothesis" for the developmental dyslexia's. *Journal of Educational Psychology*, 91(3), 1-24.

Wolf, M. & Denckla. M.B. (in press). RAN and RAS Tests. Austin, TX: Pro-Ed.

Wolf, M. & Katzir-Cohen, T. (2001). Reading fluency and its intervention. Scientific Studies of Reading. (Special Issue on Fluency. Editors: E. Kameenui & D. Simmons). 5: 211-238.

Zarillo, J. J. *Ready for RICA: A Test Preparation Guide for California's Reading Instruction Competence Assessment.* Upper Saddle River, N. J.: Prentice Hall, 2002.

About The Author

NOVA SOUTHEASTERN UNIVERSITY
Graduate Ceremony
June 16, 2007

Dr. Yvonne Simon was born on the island of Jamaica, where she received her primary and college education. She migrated to the United States and continued in the teaching profession. She attended the Nova Southeastern University in Florida, where she obtained her Bachelors of Science degree, Masters of Science degree, Specialist degree, and her Doctorate degree in education.

Dr. Simon is a life time member of the following organizations, National Education Association, American Federation of Teachers, Phi Gamma Sigma of The Fischler School of Education, and Human Services Nova Southeastern University, National Black Ph.d., and Ed.d magazine.

www.ingramcontent.com/pod-product-compliance
Lightning Source LLC
LaVergne TN
LVHW081345060426
835508LV00017B/1429

* 9 7 8 1 6 2 5 5 0 5 6 8 2 *